E AGES
entury

IGH MIDDLE AGES
n – 14th century

LATE MIDDLE AGES
13th – 15th century

THE RENAISSANCE
14th – 16th century

EARLY MODERN PERIOD
The end of the 15th century – 1648

MODERN PERIOD
1648–1918

CONTEMPORARY HISTORY
1918 – the present day

ENCYCLOPEDIA OF ORDINARY LIVING

Written by Štěpánka Sekaninová
Illustrations by Eva Chupíková

Albatros

TABLE OF CONTENTS

BATHROOM ... 4

WASHING MACHINE ... 12

KITCHEN ... 20

COOKER ... 24

REFRIGERATOR ... 30

CUTLERY ... 38

LIVING ROOM ... 44

FURNITURE ... 50

WALLPAPER ... 62

BOARD GAMES ... 68

BEDROOM ... 76

DOORS AND LOCKS ... 82

BATHROOM

After several days on the road, you are dusty, bedraggled, and dreadfully dirty. But what's the problem? Just hop in the shower or fill the tub and add bubble bath or special fragrant salts. Before you know it, you will be spanking clean and fresh as a daisy. But people didn't always have a bathroom for their immediate use at home, as we do now.

Washing in the open air

So, how did our ancestors wash? Well, they used the provisions of nature. They ducked into a cold river, pool, or stream—or the sea, if it was nearby. The luckiest among them enjoyed a refreshing shower in a sparkling waterfall. All this to a soundtrack of birdsong and the murmur of the forest, and with a warm breeze brushing their cheeks. Pretty romantic, you must admit.

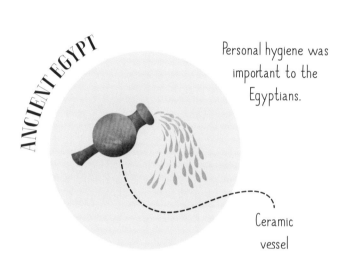

ANCIENT EGYPT

Personal hygiene was important to the Egyptians.

Ceramic vessel

The Egyptians bathed daily.

The good old bathtub

Egyptian nobility had bathtubs in their palaces, which they would use several times a day. **Warm water, supplemented with goat milk or donkey milk and scented with herbs**, was great for the skin. Rituals connected with bathing were the order of the day. Egyptians would bathe before retiring for the night, and even before meals, in the belief that the cleaner they were, the closer they were to the gods. When there was no time for a bath, a shower would do.

Timeline ⟶

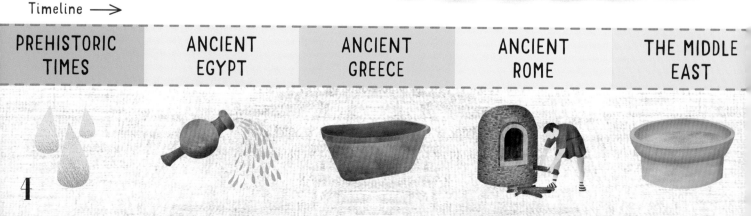

| PREHISTORIC TIMES | ANCIENT EGYPT | ANCIENT GREECE | ANCIENT ROME | THE MIDDLE EAST |

ANCIENT GREECE

Typical Greek bathtub
made of stone or clay

Hurray for the baths!

The Romans' approach to cleanliness was similar to
that of the Greeks. So it should come as no surprise
that **public baths** were very popular in Ancient Rome.
For people of the upper classes, regular visits to the
baths were practically an obligation. A communal
bath was an important social occasion. Men bathed
separately from women, of course.

Greek bathrooms

The Ancient Greeks, too, knew that **cleanliness
was next to godliness**. Whereas the poorest of the
poor maintained their personal hygiene by filling
pots with water, the wealthy bathed and washed in
special palace rooms containing **clay bathtubs and
an ingenious system of drainage**. We might say that
these were the first proper bathrooms.

The Greeks bathed regularly.

Natural sources

Public baths were fed from the natural source
of numerous hot springs. If there didn't happen
to be such a spring in the vicinity, no problem: the
Romans used aqueducts to transport warm saltwater
from distant places to their baths.

The stove for heating
water

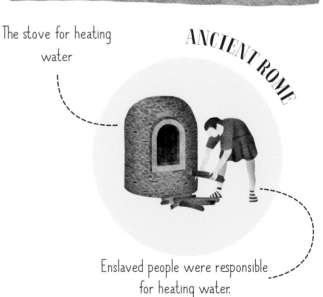

ANCIENT ROME

Enslaved people were responsible
for heating water.

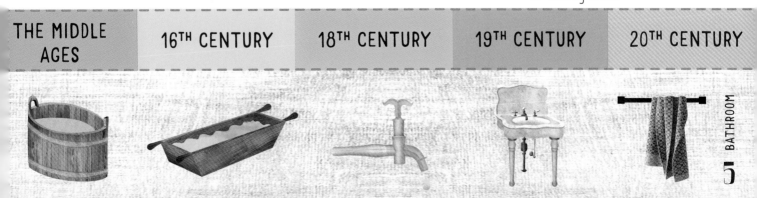

THE MIDDLE AGES	16TH CENTURY	18TH CENTURY	19TH CENTURY	20TH CENTURY

Palace bathroom

Archaeologists have found that in many Ancient Roman palaces, the wealthy had bathing pools and bathtubs with a hot-water supply. This doesn't mean, however, that these people gave up bathing in public in favor of home bathing. As we said, **public bathing was a social must**.

Bathing in the Middle East

Although the popularity and use of public baths in Ancient Rome eventually waned to nothing, the practice was copied in the Middle East and continued to flourish there. In Ancient Baghdad alone, there were around **60,000 public washrooms**.

Heated pool   Heating

In the Middle Ages, people ate at the spa as they bathed.

Timeline ⟶

PREHISTORIC TIMES	ANCIENT EGYPT	ANCIENT GREECE	ANCIENT ROME	THE MIDDLE AGES

6

Mosaic decoration

Enslaved person

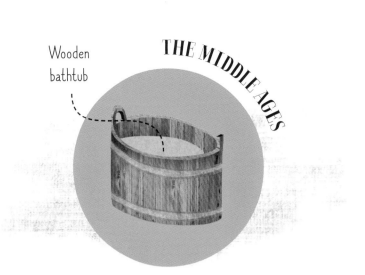

Wooden bathtub

Home bathing

What were private bathrooms like in the Middle Ages? Well, that's just it—there weren't any. Home bathing was done in the bedroom. It was enough to bring in a large wooden tub and fill it with water—which was great if you wished to hop into bed nice and clean!

Dinner in the bath

If you thought the Middle Ages were a time of dirt, think again! In the early Middle Ages, for a small fee, bathers could use **public washrooms**. There, they would discuss the matters of the day; sometimes they would even have **lunch** or **dinner**. Whereas in ancient times men bathed separately from women, in the Middle Ages everyone bathed together.

A wooden tub was a common sight in the bedroom.

People could hop out of bed and straight into the bath.

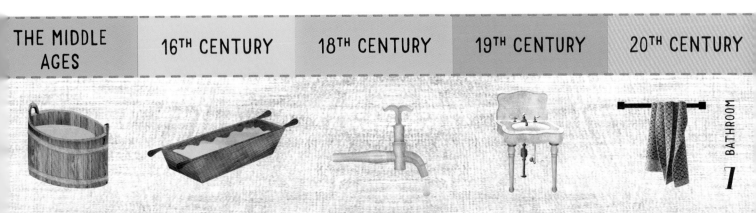

THE MIDDLE AGES	16TH CENTURY	18TH CENTURY	19TH CENTURY	20TH CENTURY

BATHROOM

7

Perfume instead of water

Owing to the ban on public bathing and the fear of the plague, people in the Middle Ages lost their desire to wash and to build home bathrooms. They believed that **clean underwear kept the body clean**, so women did an awful lot of laundry. To improve their scent, they smeared perfumed oils on themselves.

Hygiene was replaced by clean linen.

Prototype of the shower. Mr. Feetham's idea was made real by French physician François Merry Delabost.

Long live the shower!

You may wish to make note of the year 1767. This was when an Englishman named **William Feetham** invented the world's first mechanical shower. Water was pumped into a tank suspended from the ceiling. Then all you had to do was pull on a chain for a stream of water to fall on your head and gush over your body, a cue for you to burst into song. In the history of personal hygiene, this was a giant stride indeed!

The miracle of the tap

The custom of keeping one's body away from water persisted through the 17th century and into the 18th. Then came the first **sewage systems** in big cities, providing the wealthy with a **supply of fresh water** to their homes. Turn on the tap and hurray! There's running water to wash with!

Timeline ⟶

PREHISTORIC TIMES	ANCIENT EGYPT	ANCIENT GREECE	ANCIENT ROME	THE MIDDLE AGES

To the bathroom or the bedroom?

All the things we perform in the bathroom today were done in the 18th-century **bedroom**. Hands and feet would be washed in a basin on a stand in a corner of the same room where make-up was applied and hair was combed and brushed at a dressing table. All this could be done in the presence of friends and miscellaneous visitors—for what is privacy after all?

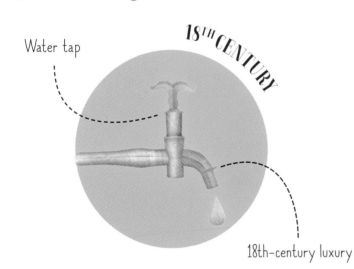

Water tap

18TH CENTURY

18th-century luxury

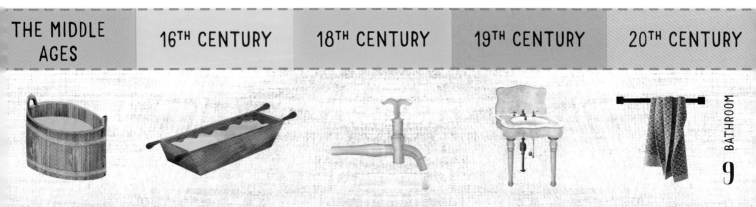

THE MIDDLE AGES	16TH CENTURY	18TH CENTURY	19TH CENTURY	20TH CENTURY

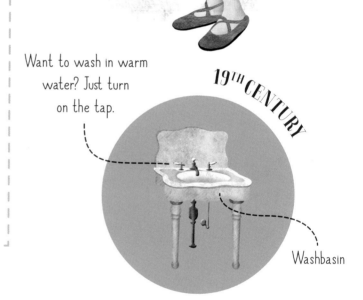

The age of hygiene

The progressive 19th century introduced many medical discoveries, and these resulted in new thinking. People rethought hygiene, this time in terms of disease prevention. Those who could afford it began to prioritize improvements to their home bathrooms. Plumbing was developed, bringing water straight to their bathtubs and washbasins, heated on its way in gas or electric heaters. Wooden tubs gave way to copper ones.

Want to wash in warm water? Just turn on the tap.

19ᵗᴴ CENTURY

Washbasin

How the poor washed

Despite their toil-filled days, poor people did find time to wash. But luxurious private bathrooms were not for them. In the tenement buildings where the poor lived, toilets and bathtubs were shared. Each time they took a bath, each member of a family had to make do with the same water as the others. The less than wealthy could also use public baths, where they would wash together under a row of showers.

Timeline ⟶

| PREHISTORIC TIMES | ANCIENT EGYPT | ANCIENT GREECE | ANCIENT ROME | THE MIDDLE AGES |

We have a bathroom too!

By the early 20th century, even homes rented by working-class families had their own bathing and toilet facilities. But these fell well short of the bathrooms of today. Before the 1960s, many families had to use an **outside toilet in a shed in the yard**. When they wished to bathe, they had to make do with a portable tub placed in front of the fire.

Our own modern century

We have seen that a bathroom of one's own was beyond the wildest dreams of most of our ancestors. Today, we can enjoy bathrooms with underfloor heating, lights that switch on and off automatically, shower heads with various water-jet options, anti-fog mirrors, you name it. So while we bathe in luxury unimaginable just a few decades ago, let us remember that in the beginning—in prehistoric times—bathing was a waterfall.

Look how lovely it is!

In the years between the First and Second World Wars, slowly but surely the importance of the bathroom continued to grow. The bathroom **became the homemaker's pride and joy** with much the same status as her kitchen. *Look at this lovely room I can relax in each evening!* she seemed to be saying to her houseguests. *Look at that gleaming bathtub, and those tiles!* And while those visitors envied her, they would dream of an even lovelier bathroom.

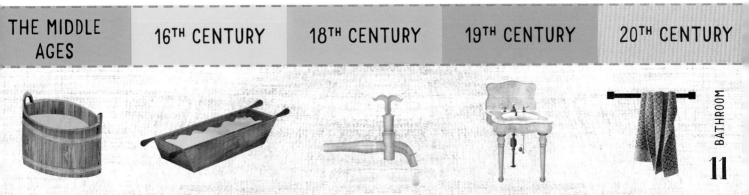

THE MIDDLE AGES	16TH CENTURY	18TH CENTURY	19TH CENTURY	20TH CENTURY

WASHING MACHINE

It often stands in the bathroom, and when it is in operation, it purrs. What is it? A washing machine, of course! A special machine that at the touch of a button turns dirty laundry into beautiful, clean, fragrant laundry. Our ancestors had a tougher time, however: for them, doing the laundry was hard labor. Let's take a look at how they did it.

A pair of Ancient Egyptians wringing out the laundry

Prehistoric laundry

Prehistoric laundry

Soon after humans took to wrapping themselves in animal skins, they were faced with a need to keep their primitive clothing clean. How did they do it? Well, they headed to the nearest **stream**, whose fresh water washed away all the dirt. They had to hold tight to their coat to make sure it wasn't washed away with the dirt.

Feet are perfect tool

Believe it or not, many Ancient Egyptians **used their feet** to do the laundry. No joke! Indeed, the hieroglyph meaning "doing laundry" shows two feet in water. People have **a lot of power in their legs**, so stomping on clothes is a great way to get dirt out.

The force of well-trained arms

Legs weren't the only limbs called into action, of course. The laundry was **twisted** and **beaten** by the hands and arms, too. As this work required greater strength, it was performed only by men. At regular intervals, they would put the whole village's laundry in special baskets, carry it to the water, and toss it in. To ensure that all dirt got out, it is said that they made use of a substance called **natron**. Whereas smaller items were washed in **tubs** made for that purpose, bed linens were carried to the **Nile**. In those days, the river was home to many crocodiles.

Timeline ⟶

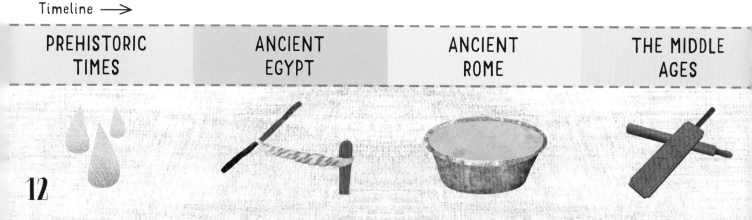

PREHISTORIC TIMES	ANCIENT EGYPT	ANCIENT ROME	THE MIDDLE AGES

Doing the laundry with urine?

The Romans had special places for doing laundry, known as **fullonicae**, providing work for strongmen known as fullones. **Fullones** would wash whatever they were given to wash. First, they would soak the laundry in a large vat, in which **bleach**, **lye**, and **urine** (yes, urine!) were added to the water. Next, they would rinse the laundry by stomping on it. Finally, they would sluice out the **cleaning agents** prior to rinsing the laundry in clean water.

ANCIENT EGYPT

Twisted laundry required strength.

A fullone uses his feet

A fullone washes laundry

Urine collection vessel

Let's use urine!

Urine contains **ammonia**, an important ingredient for washing laundry. As a result, there was a constant need for a great amount of it. But how was it delivered to the fullonicae? Quite simply, as it happens. The fullones would leave empty jars in the streets near their places of work. When someone came upon one of these jars in a moment of need, he or she could donate their water to the laundry. Long live clean, snow-white laundry!

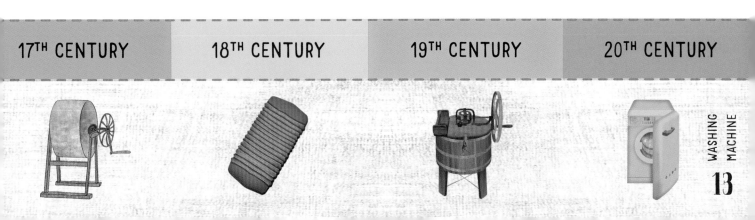

17TH CENTURY   18TH CENTURY   19TH CENTURY   20TH CENTURY

WASHING MACHINE

A big wash

In the Middle Ages, doing the laundry was an **extremely laborious** activity that could take several days to complete. It would take 15 hours just to soak the laundry; this was done in lye, which the laundresses had to keep warm. Only after this stage could the washing properly begin, with the **beating out of the dirt** with a special wooden **paddle**. This was followed by wringing and drying. It is hard to imagine that anyone looked forward to the event of doing the laundry.

Laundry dried and bleached by the sun

Beating the dirt out of laundry was a tough job.

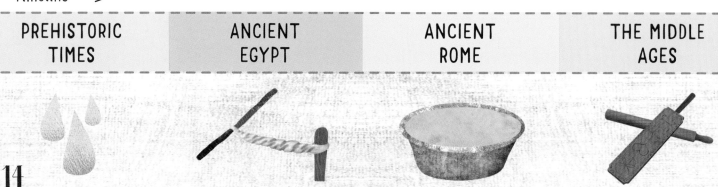

Timeline ⟶

PREHISTORIC TIMES	ANCIENT EGYPT	ANCIENT ROME	THE MIDDLE AGES

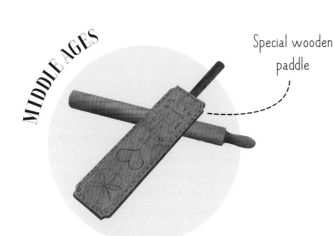

MIDDLE AGES

Special wooden paddle

Spinning drum

The year is 1691. Women are still doing their laundry on the riverbank or in a wooden tub, unaware that the day when all the effort will be removed from this activity is approaching. One of the first steps was taken by an Englishman named **John Tyzack**, inventor of the first washing machine. In fact, it was an **ordinary drum, set spinning by a hand crank**. This basic principle persists to the present day. It was a while, however, before this invention could be enjoyed by homemakers. At first, it was used only in textile factories—for washing fabrics made dirty in the production process.

A washing machine to make women's work easier remained a distant dream.

A washboard at last!

In the mid-18th century, the **washboard** first saw the light of day, bringing much relief to laundresses. Even so, they had to toil over the board, and the work still made their hands sore and bruised. A washboard could be made from one of many materials, including porcelain, stone, glass, clay, wood, and metal. Advances in technology delivered the **mechanical washboard**, which with the assistance of the laundress, would wash laundry in a rocking motion. The great disadvantage of washboards was the friction they generated, which wore out the washing very quickly.

Though a laundress tried her best, a coarse washboard could ruin her delicates.

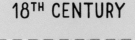

17TH CENTURY	18TH CENTURY	19TH CENTURY	20TH CENTURY

WASHING MACHINE

15

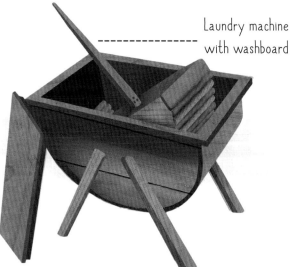

Laundry machine with washboard

Machine with washboard

Believe it or not, the ordinary washboard inspired the next step on the road to our modern way of doing laundry. An Englishman named **Stendler** invented something that made the homemaker's day a little easier—a **wooden laundry machine with a washboard**. While the laundresses rejoiced, the laundry suffered, just as it did with manually operated washboards.

Century of invention

In 1851, **James King** came up with something completely new—the **drum washing machine**. To get the drum moving, the operator only had to turn the handle. Just a few years later, in 1858, **Hamilton Smith** invented the **rotary washing machine**. Both these machines were hand-operated. Once the wash was done, the laundress had no choice but to unload the wet laundry and wring it out, a laborious task in itself.

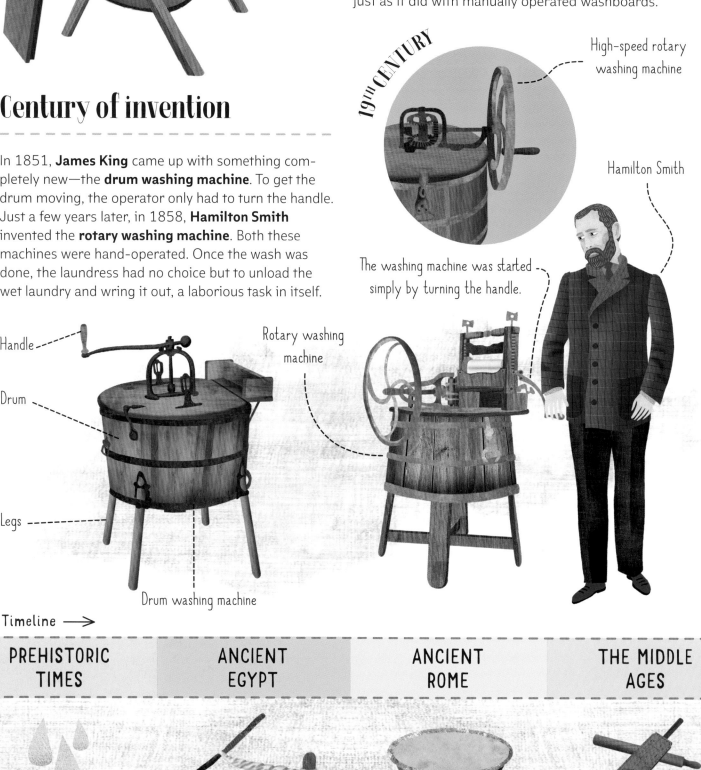

19ᵀᴴ CENTURY

High-speed rotary washing machine

Hamilton Smith

The washing machine was started simply by turning the handle.

Handle

Drum

Legs

Drum washing machine

Rotary washing machine

Timeline ⟶

PREHISTORIC TIMES	ANCIENT EGYPT	ANCIENT ROME	THE MIDDLE AGES

Hurray for electricity!

The 20th century was still getting into its stride when, in 1906, the American **Alva Fisher** invented the first **electric washing machine**. *Hurray!* By the end of that year, a significant improvement was made to it: the **water was heated in the machine itself**. That sounds pretty normal to us, doesn't it? In those days, however, it was a revolution! The first electric washing machine was a harbinger of the automatic washing machine, which first saw the light of day in 1951.

I love the smell of clean laundry!

The world's first manufacturer of washing machines

In 1874, American **William Blackstone** produced a **"high-speed rotary washing machine"** with the comfort of his own dear wife very much in his mind. Over time, this machine would find its way into many American homes. Although it washed like a dream, it had one great drawback: the water it used had to be heated in a separate container on the stove.

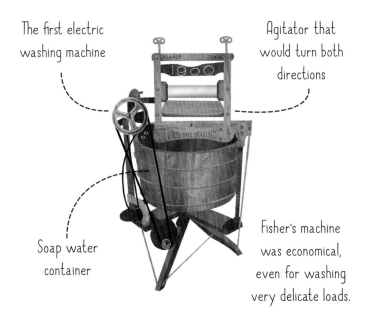

The first electric washing machine

Agitator that would turn both directions

Soap water container

Fisher's machine was economical, even for washing very delicate loads.

Washers that dry

See how far we have come from the river, the wooden washtub, the paddle, and the rough-and-ready washboard! These days, the super-modern washing machine in our home can select **how much water it needs** depending on the laundry load, **heat water to a specified temperature** to suit particular fabrics, and **gently wring out water**; some washing machines **work as driers** too.

17TH CENTURY	18TH CENTURY	19TH CENTURY	20TH CENTURY

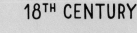

WASHING MACHINE

ADDITIONS TO BATHROOM

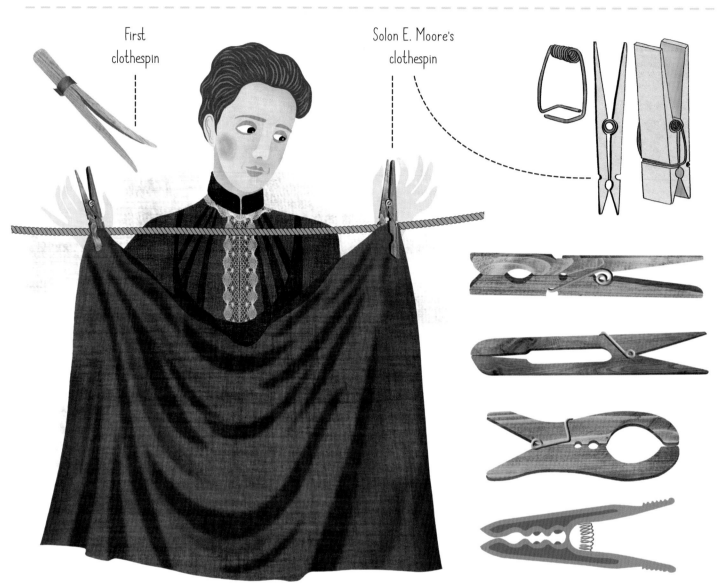

First clothespin

Solon E. Moore's clothespin

Clothespin

When we hang laundry, we secure it to the line with a clothespin to stop it from flying away. Such an ordinary thing, you might think. The first pegs were—you guessed it—wooden. They were made of a single piece of elastic wood in the shape of a V or a U. The homeland of these oldest pegs is England, their makers members of the **Christian Quaker movement**, whose devotions included small-scale handicrafts. In 1774, after a long period of persecution, the Quakers left England for America, where they continued to produce their clothespins.

Solon E. Moore

Let us stay with America and the clothespin. Having benefited from the simple Quaker clothespin, American homemakers in 1832 made use of a peg with a wooden screw. Twenty years later, **David M. Smith** from Vermont invented a **peg whose two pieces were joined by a spring**—an invention that in 1887 was improved by **Solon E. Moore** to create the peg we know today. His pegs would keep the washing on the line in the strongest wind, plus they were easy to mass produce. Thanks to Mr. Moore, the world's first clothespin factory was established.

Ironing board

Valiant **Viking women** probably used one of the **first ironing boards**. It was a pretty simple affair; laundry was placed on a flat piece of bone and pressed with heated stones. Not all that complicated, but effective nonetheless. Later, women would iron on the kitchen table, or on a board placed on two chairs. In 1858, **W. Vandenburg** and **J. Harvey** patented an ironing table for **pressing sleeves and shirts**.

The ironing board had a second, smaller board to iron sleeves and pant legs.

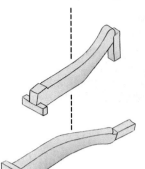

Sarah Boone

Which board is best?

Before long, there were several kinds of ironing boards to choose from. In 1875, Canadian John B. Porter came up with the first **foldable**, **portable board**, with a detachable part for pressing sleeves and pant legs. Four years later, American Albert Hogins invented the **multipurpose ironing board**, which was equipped with a special drawer for storing blankets.

And the winner is ... Sarah Boone!

The competition for best ironing board was won by **Sarah Boone**, the second African American woman to attain a patent. In 1892, she obtained a patent for a board that was narrow and slightly curved, thus facilitating the easy pressing of the more difficult-to-iron women's garments. The narrowness made it a snug fit for a sleeve or pant leg, which could then be pressed smooth on both sides. Let us say, then, that Sarah Boone is a gold medalist.

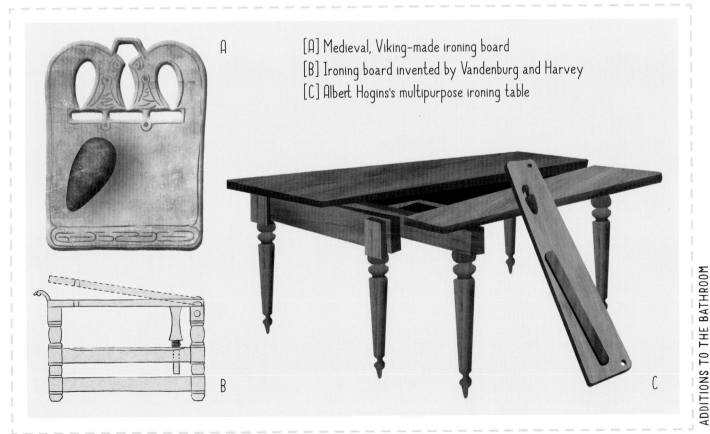

[A] Medieval, Viking-made ironing board
[B] Ironing board invented by Vandenburg and Harvey
[C] Albert Hogins's multipurpose ironing table

KITCHEN

Large or small, the kitchen is the heart of every home. In the kitchen, parents dance merrily around the cooker. While pots and pans bubble contentedly, treats and delicacies take shape. Once the magic is done, the house or flat is filled with delicious smells. It is then that Mom, Dad, and their lively little ones sit at the table and dig in. As they eat, cutlery clinks, food vanishes from the plates, and the kitchen is filled with joy and storytelling. These are everyday stories, of what has happened in the lives of Mom, Dad, and the kids on this ordinary day.

PREHISTORIC TIMES

The prehistoric way to start a fire

Cooking in prehistory

How lucky we are to have this fire, which, with a little care and attention, will serve us all year round! Prehistoric women might have said this as they checked that the mammoth roast was done right. It needs a little longer, they might have said then, as they patiently returned it to the fire. When their husbands came in from the hunt shortly afterwards, the meal was ready to serve. The very first kitchen was quite simply a fire **ring in a cave**, either at the center or hidden in a corner.

Fireplace—the prehistoric kitchen

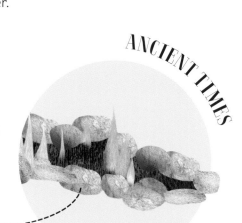

ANCIENT TIMES

Stones around a fireplace ensure that the fire doesn't spread beyond its allotted area.

Timeline ⟶

PREHISTORIC TIMES

ANTIQUITY

An ancient rarity

The homemakers of Ancient Greece had their kitchen in the **middle of the yard**, where everyone could admire it. Not only was the cooking done there; so, too, was the eating. In antiquity, the kitchen was surrounded on all sides by the house's other rooms. The reason for this was purely practical: first, it was easy to reach for all who lived there; second, the heat produced by the cooking **kept every space in the house**—from the master bedroom to the guest rooms—**nice and warm**. But if you think every house had a kitchen, you are mistaken. Not everyone could afford such luxury. There were large kitchens on the edges of Greek cities used by the general public.

EARLY MIDDLE AGES

LATE MIDDLE AGES

Black kitchens

How smoky it is in here! Guess which period we find ourselves in? That's right, this kitchen is in the early Middle Ages. It has an **open fireplace and a hole in the ceiling where we might expect a chimney**. This explains the smoke-stained walls. In the manor houses of the time, this grimy room was kept out of sight. In the dwellings of ordinary people, who were crammed into a single room, the kitchen took up a small space between the fireplace and the door.

Timeline ⟶

PREHISTORIC TIMES

ANTIQUITY

A chimney in the house made things much nicer for the cook, as it kept the kitchen clean and cozy. In the 19th century or thereabouts, the kitchen gained a stove, to which were later added a refrigerator, a water supply, and a waste pipe. From the mid-20th century on, kitchens underwent rapid modernization. Kitchens of today have very little in common with the open fires and smoke-stained walls of yesteryear!

Hurray for the chimney!

In the later Middle Ages, people put a **chimney** in their roof. This allowed them to enclose their fires in an **oven** or a **furnace** in the corner of the room. The kitchen of a noble family was a presentable room with a separate dining room. But what about ordinary, poor people? Well, the neediest among them would be cooking over an open fireplace in a smoky kitchen space for centuries yet; for them, chimneys were the stuff of dreams.

EARLY MIDDLE AGES

LATE MIDDLE AGES

COOKER

The prehistoric cooker was basically a **fireplace**. It was set either in a slight depression in the ground or within a ring of stones. Initially, the only function of such a fireplace in the heart of a cave was to provide heat. It was first used to heat food around 100 BCE. Before long, prehistoric humans came up with more sophisticated uses for fire as they learned to tame it for their needs. For instance, they would lay slices of meat wrapped in **green leaves** in the **fireplace depression** on a layer of hot stones—to delicious effect.

Meat was laid on heated stones, at the edge. The roast soon smelled delicious.

Hot stones

PREHISTORIC TIMES

Clay oven ipnos

Timeline →

Fire at the heart of the home

The oven, cooker, or stove—whatever you wish to call it—remained as an arrangement of stones around a **fireplace** for a long time. It was given pride of place at the center of the dwelling. Cooking pots were laid on stones. The cook had all she needed near at hand. Such a stove might appear primitive at first glance, but it was used to boil, bake, fry, and smoke food. What more could a cook ask for!

24

PREHISTORIC TIMES	ANCIENT GREECE	ANCIENT ROME	THE MIDDLE AGES

ANCIENT GREECE

Portable oven

Baking in ancient times

Human development continued in leaps and bounds, and progress was reflected in kitchen appliances. Take a look for yourself at Ancient Greece, where women prepared meals in **ipnos** clay ovens, which were heated with wood. The **portable oven** was another innovation from Ancient Greece—from way back in the 17th century BCE!

Inspired by the Greeks

The Ancient Romans drew inspiration from Greece when equipping their kitchens. Some of the solid ovens they built from stone, brick, and ceramics have survived to the present.

The ruins of a bakery in the Roman city of Pompeii

| 5TH – 16TH CENTURY | 18TH CENTURY | 19TH CENTURY | PRESENT DAY |

 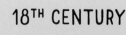   

COOKER

25

Cauldron

On top of the Russian stove

In the 15th and 16th centuries, households welcomed the so-called Russian stove. Not only was **cooking** done in it, but it also **provided heat for the whole room**—and those who so wished could even **sleep** on top of it. There's nothing better than being lovely and warm at night.

The good old cauldron

In the Middle Ages, all cooking was done on an **open kitchen fire**. Pots with lids were placed on a trivet in the fireplace. If there was no trivet, a **cauldron** on legs was used instead. Alternately, pots were suspended over the fire and the cooking could go on like that till the cows came home. If the weather was nice, everyone was glad to move operations to the outdoor fireplace. You can imagine that food prepared in the open air to the sound of birdsong tasted a hundred times better. In the Middle Ages, an oven was used for bread-making only.

Timeline ⟶

PREHISTORIC TIMES	ANCIENT GREECE	ANCIENT ROME	THE MIDDLE AGES

Benjamin Thompson — Kitchener — William Flavell

The improved, Rumford fireplace, with a single source of fire at its center.

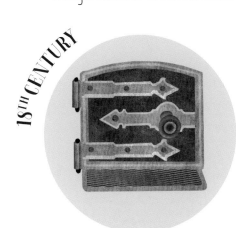

18TH CENTURY

18th century inventors

For a long time, stoves and ovens remained much as they were. In the 18th century, however, a certain Count Rumford invented the kitchen range and potato soup too! Rumford—whose birth name was **Benjamin Thompson**—improved the cast-iron stove to such a degree that a single source of fire could **heat several pots at once**, all the while **keeping the room warm**. The cook could regulate the temperature under each pot and pan as needed. The only drawback was that it took up so much space that only those with a large kitchen could install it.

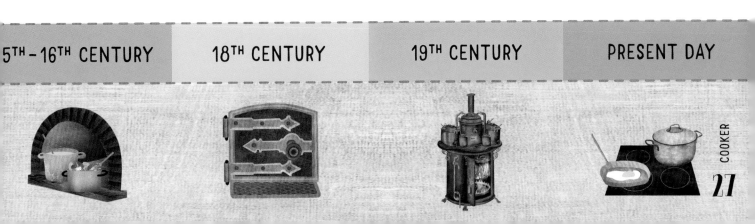

5TH–16TH CENTURY | 18TH CENTURY | 19TH CENTURY | PRESENT DAY

COOKER

27

Century of steam

Count Rumford's invention surely did much to inspire **William Flavel**. In 1830, Flavel launched the super-modern **Kitchener** range. Made of cast iron, it fed on solid fuel. Like Rumford's range, the Kitchener could boil, bake, fry, and heat from a single source, all at once. Flavel's range was smaller than Rumford's, however, allowing keepers of smaller kitchens to dance merrily around the room while they worked.

Thomas Ahearn

Gas stove

Long live natural gas!

The name of **James Sharp** is one you will wish to remember. James Sharp was a factory owner who loved his wife very much—so much, in fact, that he invented a gas stove in her honor. Rather than continue to hear her complaints about how black coal dirtied her hands, he took the matter into his own, so to speak. From 1825 on, Mrs. Sharp cooked happily on her husband's invention, her hands squeaky clean. But many of her contemporaries were less impressed with it. Not only was gas an explosion hazard, but by the standards of the day it was terribly expensive.

19TH CENTURY

Sharp's gas stove

Timeline ⟶

PREHISTORIC TIMES	ANCIENT GREECE	ANCIENT ROME	THE MIDDLE AGES

Tamed lightning

After Canadian Thomas Ahearn presented his new electric cooker to the world in 1883, excitable journalists wrote that supper was prepared by "tamed lightning." Just a few years later, in 1908, this appliance underwent a few minor adjustments at the hands of Emil Rathenau; soon after that, it became a feature in most forward-thinking households.

A modern kitchen

In our own ultramodern age, gleaming cookers show off their perfection. Those who prefer gas can delight in an **all-gas cooker.** Those who can't make up their minds may choose a **combo cooker**, with a gas-powered stovetop and an electric oven. Fans and lovers of electricity can opt for an **all-electric cooker.** I wonder what homemakers of ancient and medieval times would have made of all this choice.

5TH – 16TH CENTURY	18TH CENTURY	19TH CENTURY	PRESENT DAY

REFRIGERATOR

We keep yogurt, cheese, milk, fruit juice, eggs, ice cream, together with other good things to eat and drink that need to be kept cold, in a well-ordered refrigerator. A fridge is a kind of magic box that is an integral part of every single kitchen today. How else could we keep our groceries fresh? How else could we keep them from spoiling? It may seem to us an ordinary thing, but a fridge is a great invention that we couldn't do without. So how did people keep food chilled in the dim and distant past?

PREHISTORIC TIMES

Meat and fruit were stored in cold caves.

But what about meat?

Our earliest ancestors had to work hard for the food they ate. They **hunted, dug up** roots, **gathered** wild fruit and chomped nuts. Fortune didn't always smile on them: times of plenty alternated with times of hunger. Feast and famine. They learned to deal with this by creating stores for winter **in imitation** of their animal friends. Stored nuts will last a long time. But what about meat? This was a recurring problem for prehistoric humans, which they may have solved by chance. Stored at the very back of the cave, which was its **coldest part**, a mammoth rump would last longer than if stored closer to the fire.

Chilled supplies were important on days when food was scarce.

ANCIENT PERSIA

Timeline ⟶

PREHISTORIC TIMES	ANCIENT PERSIA	ANCIENT CHINA	THE MIDDLE AGES

Ancient cooling pits

By the time of antiquity, people knew more about keeping food cool, and they behaved accordingly. The Ancient Persians built the first cold stores: special **chambers dug into the ground**, which they filled with ice and snow. The longer these remained in their frozen state, the longer the food packed along with them was preserved. In the middle of the desert in the scorching Persian summer, you can imagine the benefits of this. The cooling system used was more than simple. Channels in these ancient refrigerators **held water from thawed snow and ice**, which evaporated to **keep the fridge's contents cool.**

Cold stores had to be regularly supplied with ice—a rarity.

Ice and wells

The Ancient Chinese, too, used ice to chill their food. They kept the ice in special containers, which were at first **ceramic** and later made of **copper**. And where did the Ancient Chinese go for their ice? Well, every December, like clockwork, a special unit of 80 soldiers set out for snowy climes, where they chopped away at and gathered as much ice as they could carry. Unlike the wealthy ruling classes, poorer folk could not afford a neat "fridge." They kept their food stores chilled in **wells**, in baskets lowered to the bottom on ropes. Hardly rocket science, but very effective.

The Ancient Greeks and Romans, too, were quick to understand the benefits of keeping food cool. They kept imported ice in boxes which they stored in pits lined with wood and straw for insulation. Used in this way, the ice thawed very slowly.

ANCIENT CHINA

The advantage of the cellar

In the Middle Ages, food was kept cool in extensive **cellars and large underground rooms**. Stores were packed in ice and snow gathered in the winter months for use in spring and summer. As for special rooms lined with ice all year round, these were no longer as popular as they had been in ancient times, not least because they were expensive to maintain; only a rich man could engage a caravan of merchants to travel great distances for the precious, scarce commodity of ice. Cellars **deep in the ground** were a simpler, far cheaper solution.

Timeline ⟶

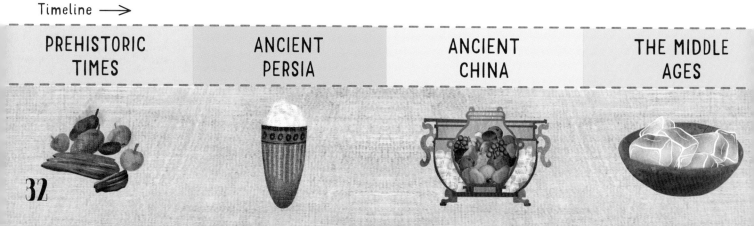

| PREHISTORIC TIMES | ANCIENT PERSIA | ANCIENT CHINA | THE MIDDLE AGES |

So what did people who weren't rich do when they wished to keep milk and meat fresh for future use? Some built a special wooden shed close to the site of a spring, storing food in the cold water, thus keeping it fresh and unspoiled for longer.

Ice pits

It was enough to find a spot on a riverbank which didn't get much sunlight, dig a pit there, and line the pit with sawdust and ice. Meat and other perishable food tended to do very well down there. At a castle, such an icehouse would take the form of an extensive cellar. Wealthy townspeople of this period enjoyed the use of luxury freezers, special boxes that would be filled with ice by tradesmen known as "icemen."

THE MIDDLE AGES

Ice supplies for food storage

REFRIGERATOR

First artificial freezing in the world

In the early 18th century, Scottish physician and chemist **William Cullen**, a well-traveled man of the Enlightenment, was determined to figure out how to freeze food without importing expensive ice from high mountains. He finally came up with a special appliance, which was **cooled** to form **crystals** of artificial **ice** by the turning of a crank. The simple refrigerator was composed of a pump that compressed diethyl ether, a colorless, flammable liquid with a low boiling point.

William Cullen with his simple refrigerator

William Cullen 1710–1790

Oliver Evans 1755–1819

Evans's proposal, the first refrigerator, was never realized!

later, the first fridge was produced, by **James Harrison**. That incredible ice machine could produce almost **three tons of ice a day**—so hats off to Mr. Harrison! It had one serious drawback, however: it was so large and bulky that to place it in a kitchen was unthinkable. It could be installed only in a factory hall.

James Harrison 1816–1893

If you like, I'll make you a cube THIS big!

First refrigerator

"What a useful thing a proper refrigerator would be!" said the American **Oliver Evans** in 1805. And he set about designing the world's very first. Unfortunately, Evans's fridge never saw the light of day. Fifty years

Timeline ⟶

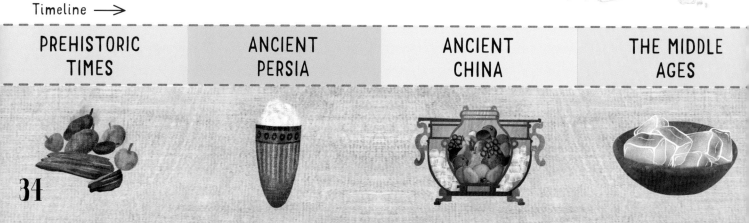

| PREHISTORIC TIMES | ANCIENT PERSIA | ANCIENT CHINA | THE MIDDLE AGES |

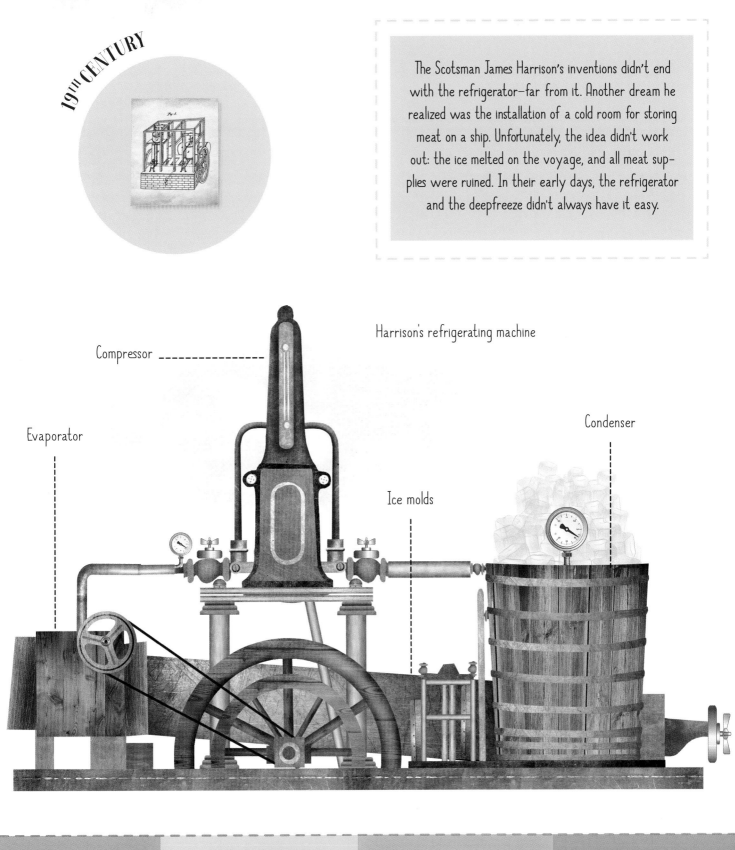

The Scotsman James Harrison's inventions didn't end with the refrigerator—far from it. Another dream he realized was the installation of a cold room for storing meat on a ship. Unfortunately, the idea didn't work out: the ice melted on the voyage, and all meat supplies were ruined. In their early days, the refrigerator and the deepfreeze didn't always have it easy.

Compressor

Harrison's refrigerating machine

Evaporator

Condenser

Ice molds

18ᵀᴴ CENTURY	19ᵀᴴ CENTURY	20ᵀᴴ CENTURY	PRESENT DAY

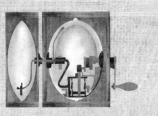
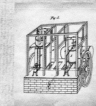

Harrison is not everyone's champion of refrigeration, however. In the 1870s, German engineer and scientist Carl von Linde designed a reliable cooling apparatus based on the use of compressed ammonia. As a result, many consider him the inventor of the cooling system.

A huge and loud compressor was not practical.

Refrigerator

Compressor

A Big Breakthrough

The 20th century had barely begun when the **fridge** came along at last. From 1911 on, the richest of the rich took this innovation into their home and hoisted it up in the kitchen, where it looked splendid as it froze and chilled. The problem was, the **compressor** of sulfur dioxide, which kept the box cool, was too loud. To minimize the disturbance, it was consigned to the basement.

Timeline ⟶

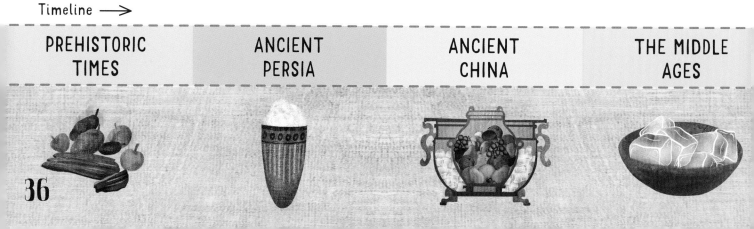

| PREHISTORIC TIMES | ANCIENT PERSIA | ANCIENT CHINA | THE MIDDLE AGES |

America versus Europe

Although **Frigidaire refrigerators** were an integral part of the ordinary American household from the 1930s on, the European fridge boom had a few more decades to wait. Not until the **1970s** was the fridge a common feature of the European kitchen. Before then, people relied on ice from the iceman, just as their ancestors had.

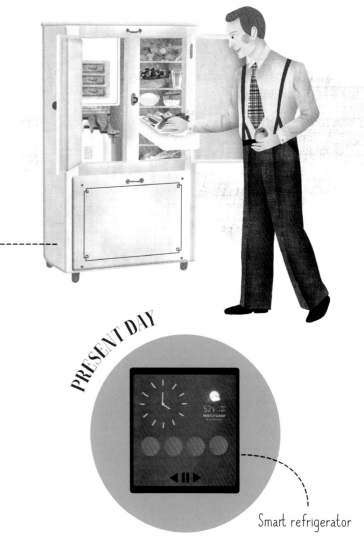

Frigidaire ---------

Modern fridge

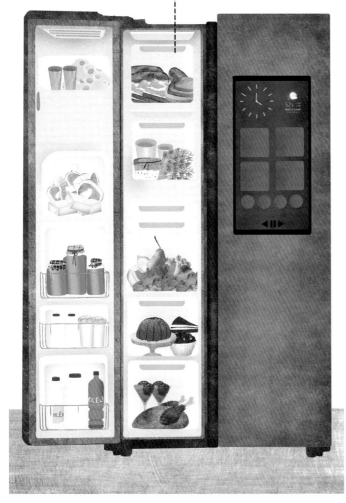

PRESENT DAY

Smart refrigerator

21st-century progress

Today's ultramodern fridges look something like this. What would households in prehistory, the Middle Ages, and the Age of Steam make of them? I reckon they would be flabbergasted. This fridge has a touch-screen that will buy your groceries for you. It will even keep you entertained while you cook, as it has a built-in video player. But it is less romantic than blocks of ice, cold rooms in cellars, and cooling streams, as I'm sure you would agree.

18ᵀᴴ CENTURY	19ᵀᴴ CENTURY	20ᵀᴴ CENTURY	PRESENT DAY

CUTLERY

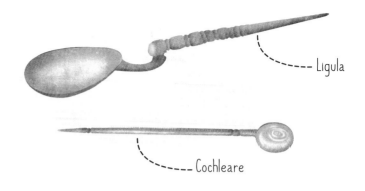

Ligula

Cochleare

What kind of madman decided it would be a good idea to make eating more complicated? Wouldn't it be more fun to chase your noodles around the soup bowl with your fingers? Plus, there are still some cultures that use their hands for eating and don't understand why Westerners insist on making our lives more difficult. On the other hand, where did forks and knives even come from? What's the story behind cutlery?

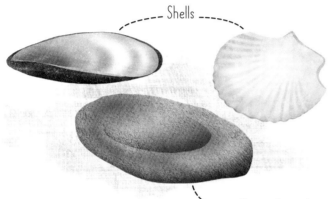

Shells

Spoon from stone

The spoon is the winner

Because it was the spoon that preceded all other cutlery. Originally, it didn't look like modern spoons. People used to ladle up water with **shells** and or with hollows in **stones** or **bones**. Simply put, they used anything that could hold at least some of the delicious liquid. It was no luxury, indeed, and lacked any handle that would allow you to scoop up a very hot meal. Handles were added to spoons only in Ancient Egypt, but were used mostly for rituals rather than eating.

One isn't enough

Ancient Romans wouldn't be satisfied with a single type of spoon. Why not go the whole hog and have two kinds? One, called **ligula**, was shaped like a pear and was great for ladling up soups or thin porridges. The other one—**the cochleare**—was smaller and Romans ate eggs or mollusks with it.

A Chinese gadget

The Ancient Chinese used the spoon to eat, and it was a great tool! That's because Chinese inventors made it pointy. Why, you ask? The sharp tip was very useful when one needed to scoop up a tough morsel.

Wooden, or golden?

Medieval spoons were made from **wood, brass, tin, horn**, and even **silver** and **gold**. One look at the material was all it took for one to immediately know who used what. The poor were lucky if they could eat with wooden, brass, tin, or horn spoons, while aristocrats gorged themselves full with silver ones. Meanwhile, the royals wouldn't be happy if they had to eat with anything that wasn't pure gold.

Tin   Silver   Wood   Gold

The knife places second

As early as prehistoric times, people made the first **knives—sharp fragments of flint, bone, or obsidian**. Originally, people could do without a handle, but then added one anyway. No wonder—it made chopping stuff much easier. So what was in such a pressing need of being chopped to pieces? Big chunks of meat, of course!

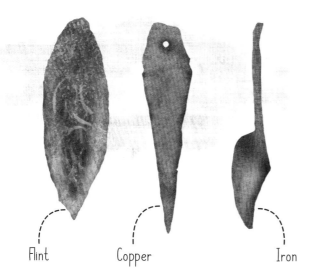

Flint   Copper   Iron

No life without a knife

The Middle Ages favored small knives, tucked neatly behind one's belt. People would sit down at the table, take the knife out, and start eating. Watch out, guys! Don't cut yourselves! And because the feasters sometimes did cut themselves, Louis XIV, the famous 17th-century French ruler, banned sharped knives from being used for eating. But since food still had to be cut somehow, a simple solution emerged: the **tip was made round**.

The knife—a useful helper

Hurray for the fork!

On the other hand, there was something to sharp tips. They served the same purpose as the sharp handle of the Chinese fork—to stab all conceivable and inconceivable goodies. What a good thing that people came up with the fork. What would we do if they hadn't? This is no talon, just an ordinary fork. Well, a fork made in Ancient Egypt, that is. It was a great tool for any cook who needed something to pull meat out of hot water.

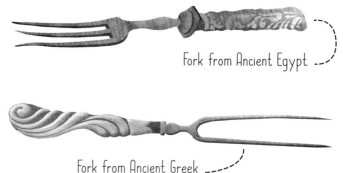

Fork from Ancient Egypt

Fork from Ancient Greek

From the Middle East to Southern Europe

Ancient Greeks and Romans enjoyed the advantages of the fork—this time, a **large two-pointed one**. It was great for putting food into bowls. But when and where were forks first used for eating? In the 4th-century Byzantine Empire. From there, the fork came to the Middle East. The two-pointed fork was successful wherever it went. When a Roman emperor tried it out at the end of the 10th century, he was quite impressed. And so it settled in Italy.

From Italy, and on and on ...

From Italy, the fork moved to **France** and then all the way up to **Northern Europe**, where tough guys resisted for a pretty long time. It wasn't until the 18th century that they gave in and the fork finally earned its rightful place at the table. It had to win over not only regular folk, but also church dignitaries! Well, you see, the fork does rather look like a devil's pitchfork. The original historic forks were either two- or three-pointed. The four prongs we favor today didn't appear until the 19th century.

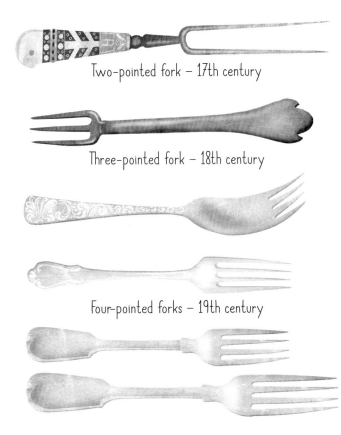

Two-pointed fork – 17th century

Three-pointed fork – 18th century

Four-pointed forks – 19th century

Tablecloth

Cutlery looks good when placed on a tablecloth. But originally, in ancient times, tables were bare. To wipe their greasy hands clean, diners carried cloth napkins around—the so-called mappae. **In the 9th century, tables started to be covered with leather or parchment cloths.** Three more centuries had to pass before these hard materials were replaced with woolen carpets. Then, the carpets took a back seat in favor of canvas, and the first tablecloths were born—ones that resemble what we can see in modern dining rooms today.

A medieval feast

Straw

Two men are holding a glass and slurping its contents happily. This image of two drinkers would be nothing to write home about, if it didn't originate in about 3,000 BCE. Archaeologists discovered it in a Sumerian tomb, along with rare golden straws decorated with gemstones. Over the centuries, it was more common for people to sip their beverages with plant straws—like culms. The drawback? They couldn't withstand the pressure of the liquid and would fall apart directly in your mouth. Fortunately, **Marvin Chester**, a 19th-century American, made the very first waxed paper tube. Comfortable drinking guaranteed.

Chopsticks

Chopsticks are quite old—they were first used as early as **5,000 ago**, in **Ancient China**. Why go for them, exactly? Imagine that you're cooking some meat and would like to take it out. But how could you when it's so hot! But then, bamboo is growing all around. So what do you do? You break off two bamboo twigs and use them to take the meat out, no problem. While aristocrats and noblemen ate with sticks made from nephrite, gold, and silver, common people were more than grateful for bamboo and wood.

Joseph B. Friedman

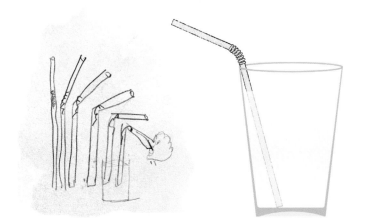

Differences between chopsticks

Chinese chopsticks are longer and their tips are round rather than pointed. Meanwhile, Japanese chopsticks are shorter and pointier.

Chinese chopsticks

Japanese chopsticks

Bendy Straws

By a stroke of luck, another American—**Joseph B. Friedman**—had a small daughter who loved milk and wouldn't let her straw out of her hands. After all, it was so much fun to drink with! But not very comfortable sometimes—what if you were too small and the straw too long? You almost had to stand on your tiptoes to reach. But Friedman was a practical man. He put a screw into the straw and wrapped a piece of dental floss around its thread, thus creating the first ever bendy straw!

KITCHEN-EXTRAS

In the beginning was the can

For the invention of the tin-can opener, the invention of the tin can itself had to come first. It was the end of the 18th century and war was raging in Europe. The brilliant French military commander Napoleon was trying to figure out how to achieve a ready supply of good, fresh food to his large army. It took 15 years to find the answer. It was provided by a Parisian confectioner named Nicolas Appert, who simply put a cooked lunch in a glass jar and stoppered it with a cork. England, France's enemy, responded to the culinary challenge, however. In the very same year, the workshop of **Peter Durand** replaced glass with the first tin cans.

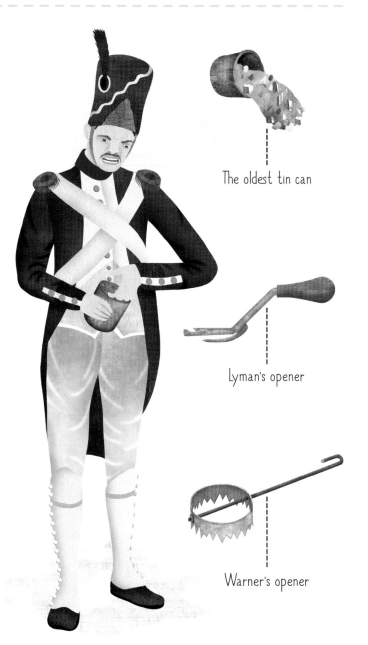

The oldest tin can

Lyman's opener

Warner's opener

Back to the opener

So now we had the cans. But the question remained: how to crack them open. Hungry soldiers attacked them with knives, stones, bayonets, and—if nothing else would do the trick—they would shoot off the lid. When your tummy is rumbling, there is no time for niceties. In 1858, **Ezra Warner** of America invented the first truly practical can opener. A tool whose tip had a curved blade performed the job with aplomb. But there was a problem: it could be terribly hard on the fingers. In 1870, a somewhat safer can opener first saw the light of day; invented by **William Lyman**, it replaced the sharp blade with a little wheel.

19th century

1891

The pressure cooker is a thick-walled container that boils at pressures above the existing atmospheric pressure. This high pressure makes it possible to achieve temperatures within the container of up to 260 °F, so that food can be cooked or stewed more quickly. Foods prepared in a pressure cooker have a more distinctive taste.

A pressure cooker and an enthusiastic inventor

These days, many households contain a pressure cooker, a little device that comes to a boil super-fast and whose high pressure works wonders ... But did you know that the very first pressure cooker was designed as a steam engine to supply one of Louis XIV's fountains with fresh water? That's right—this is what inventor **Denis Papin** came up with in the 17th century. In the process, he also invented the type of pressurized pot that no modern cook can do without. Papin discovered that the higher the pressure in the pot, the sooner the food within it is cooked, while retaining all its taste and nutrients. To think, all this began as a commission for King Louis XIV!

Electric kettle

I need a cup of hot tea right now! Just as well, then, that I have an electric kettle, which will boil the water for the tea in the blink of an eye. Can you believe that **the first attempts to boil water at high speed were made in ancient times**, in Mesopotamia? It was in this region that archaeologists discovered a receptacle resembling a kettle from the period between 3,500 BCE and 2,000 BCE. But let us move on to 17th-century England, where the beautiful silver teapot first appeared at tea parties. The electric kettle did not begin its era of dominance until the late 19th century, however. And—let us be honest—the first ones were anything but fast; indeed, the water in them took 12 minutes to reach a boil. Not until 1922 was a heating element built into the kettle, thus accelerating the boiling process. The technology of the electric kettle truly came into its own in the 1950s.

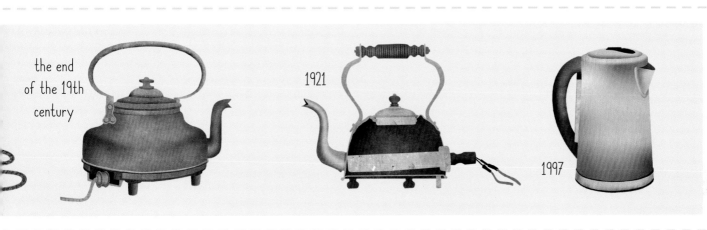

the end of the 19th century

1921

1997

LIVING ROOM

Let us go into the living room to watch our favorite children's TV show. The living room is the place for playing board games and chatting all afternoon with guests over tea and cakes. The living room is the beating heart of every home. It is also where Dad lies on the sofa to catch 40 winks and ends up catching hundreds. But what about our ancestors? Did they, too, have living rooms in their homes?

Living room and kitchen in one.

A slightly higher level of protection against the desert sand.

Comfortable cave

One cave with one fireplace, around which the whole gang is gathered. As we know, the prehistoric cave was **the kitchen, living room, storeroom,** and **bedroom** all rolled into one. Does that mean that our distant ancestors had no privacy? Well, why wouldn't they? They spent most of their time outside, where there is room enough to be alone.

Egyptian living

Wealthy Egyptians painted the brick walls of their houses white, so as not to attract the sun. These houses contained up to 30 rooms. Although most were storage rooms, there were also nurseries, bathrooms, bedrooms, and yes, living rooms. The Egyptian living room was at the very **center** of the house, surrounded by all the other rooms, thus ensuring that it remained nice and cool in summer and plenty warm enough in winter. The floor of the living room—where all socializing in the house was done—was on a **slightly higher level**, a protection against the desert sand, which got everywhere. No one likes the constant crunch of grains of sand under their feet.

Timeline ⟶

| PREHISTORIC TIMES | ANCIENT EGYPT | ANCIENT GREECE | ANCIENT ROME |

The chair—an integral part of living rooms.

ANCIENT EGYPT

Greek comfort

And how about the Ancient Greeks? Did they, too, have living rooms? In their comfortable homes, everything was concentrated around a **central courtyard**. Without the permission of their husbands, women could not go about outdoors as they pleased, so they would sit in this yard, chatting and enjoying the fresh air. Otherwise, they would spend their time in areas of the house designated for their use, while the men were in the dining rooms.

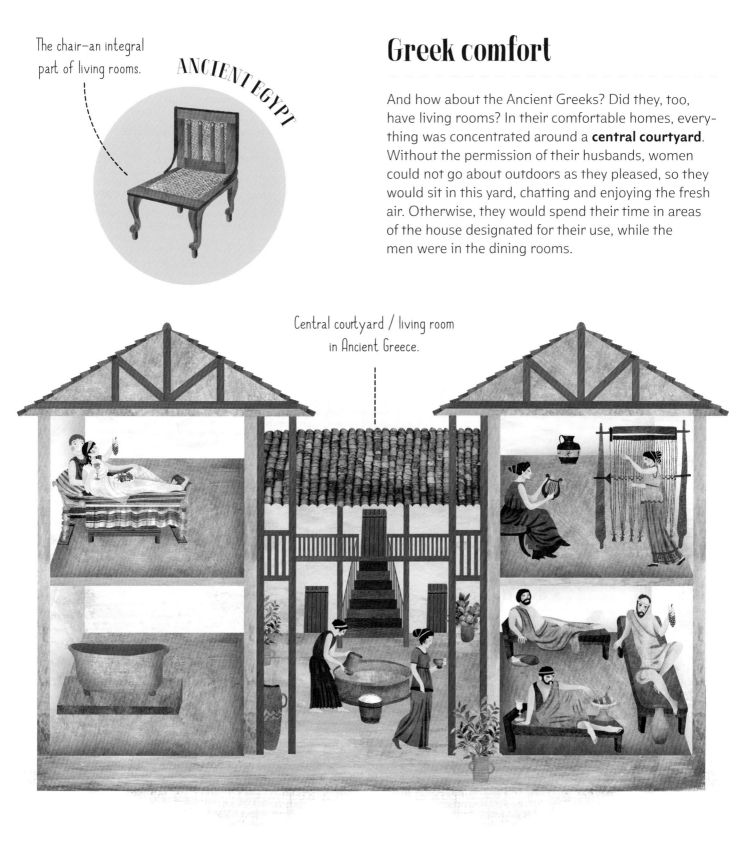

Central courtyard / living room in Ancient Greece.

| THE MIDDLE AGES | 17TH – 18TH CENTURY | 19TH CENTURY | 20TH CENTURY |

Roman triclinum

Tablinum and triclinum

Wealthy Romans lived in luxury in beautiful villas. The Roman living room equivalent was a space known as the **tablinum**. It was connected to a roofed court-yard known as an **atrium**, which was where guests were received. Sometimes the tablinum would function as the office of the master of the house. The most presentable room in the house was the dining room, known as the **triclinum**. This contained couches on which hosts and guests would recline as they dined and conversed.

ANCIENT ROME

In Ancient Rome, beds were places for feasting as well as resting.

Timeline ⟶

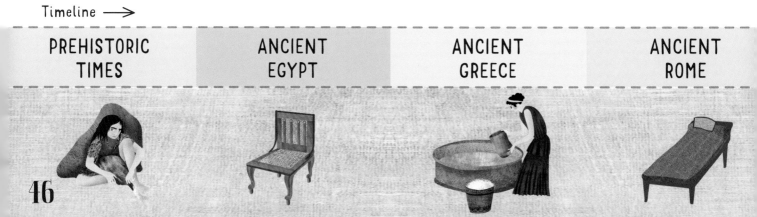

| PREHISTORIC TIMES | ANCIENT EGYPT | ANCIENT GREECE | ANCIENT ROME |

46

Posh armchair

In the Middle Ages, too, the rich had their living rooms. These were places not only for relaxing but also for showing off wealth and power. In early medieval times, the main focus of the living room was an armchair in which the master of the house would sit in proud comfort while his servants busied themselves around him or sat on low stools waiting for his instructions. **The master would also sit in his high armchair when he received guests.** It wasn't difficult to understand what he meant this to show: Look at me! See how high and mighty I am!

A luxurious room of the 17th century.

THE MIDDLE AGES	17ᵀᴴ–18ᵀᴴ CENTURY	19ᵀᴴ CENTURY	20ᵀᴴ CENTURY

Showing off your living room

In the 17th century, living rooms became **showcases of family life**, rather than special places for receiving guests, thus allowing proud homeowners to demonstrate that they had many rooms. These new living rooms were adorned with expensive art and equipped with the best furniture; if the family was a noble one, a coat of arms would be displayed. All important events in the life of the family—most notably weddings, birthdays, and wakes—would be celebrated in the living room.

17ᵀᴴ – 18ᵀᴴ CENTURY

Children not allowed

Today, families **come together** in the living room. In the late 19th century, however, it was known as the drawing room and used only to receive guests. Children were not even allowed in; after all, who would wish to risk damage to their precious furniture, patterned carpets, and expensive china? The family came together in other rooms of the house. Not only would homeowners receive visitors in their **finest room**, but they would do so in their best clothes.

Timeline ⟶

PREHISTORIC TIMES	ANCIENT EGYPT	ANCIENT GREECE	ANCIENT ROME

Drawing rooms for the dead

Many people died in battle in the First World War. Many more died shortly thereafter, as a result of a terrible flu pandemic. For a time, the drawing room became the place where the body of the departed was laid out for other members of the family to mourn. Only once the reverberations of war and deadly disease had faded did drawing rooms resume their social function. Before long, they became known as **living rooms**.

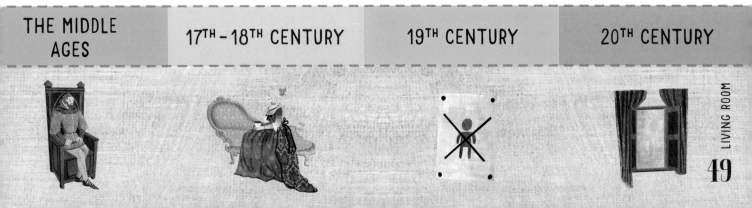

THE MIDDLE AGES

17TH – 18TH CENTURY

19TH CENTURY

20TH CENTURY

FURNITURE

Can you imagine a room without furniture? I mean any room—a living room, nursery, dining room, bedroom, study room, guest room, you name it. All rooms are dominated by furniture, most notably cupboards, chairs, tables, and desks. These might be modern, designer, retro, new, or hand-me-down from beloved grandparents ... But do we know how furniture originated, or how it has developed over time? Let us take a closer look.

Stone Age

Even in the age when former hunter-gatherers settled into a life of agriculture, primitive dwellings were improved with furniture. Naturally, it was made of stone, for this was the Stone Age. The benches, chests, cupboards, and beds made in a Scottish village on the Orkney Islands between 3,100—2,450 BCE were all made of stone (as discovered by archaeologists).

Timeline ⟶

| PREHISTORIC TIMES | ANCIENT EGYPT | MESOPOTAMIA | ANCIENT GREECE | ANCIENT ROME | THE MIDDLE AGES |

Pharaoh's throne

As for the Egyptian pharaoh, he would sit in comfortable splendor on a throne, with a stool under his feet. Only the most important Egyptians sat in a chair like this. The royal footstool was decorated with pictures of Egypt's enemies, so that the pharaoh could step on them, at least symbolically.

Portable furniture

Paintings and engravings on walls provide us with clear evidence that the Ancient Egyptians enjoyed the luxury of furniture. Their **beds, stools, chairs, small tables**, and **chests** were all characterized by subtle simplicity, lightness, and ease of storage. The Egyptians had no fondness for heavy, bulky pieces—not only for aesthetic reasons but because a shortage of good-quality wood for sturdy furniture meant that it had to be imported from further afield. Egyptian cabinetmakers deftly adorned their pieces with ivory, glass, gold leaf, silver leaf, and precious stones.

ANCIENT EGYPT

14TH – 15TH CENTURY   16TH CENTURY   THE BAROQUE PERIOD   18TH CENTURY   19TH – 20TH CENTURY   PRESENT DAY

FURNITURE

51

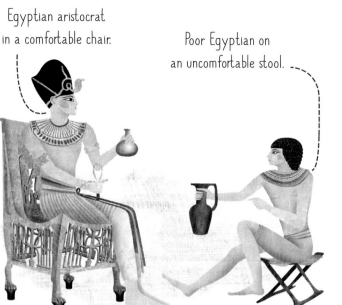

Egyptian aristocrat in a comfortable chair.

Poor Egyptian on an uncomfortable stool.

Rich man, poor man

While the Egyptian poor had to make do with **storage chests** made of **reeds**, their rich compatriots, who liked to show off their wealth, filled their homes with chests with splendid painted decorations, ornate armchairs whose four legs were carved in animal designs (commonly lion's paws), low tables of expensive ebony or sycamore wood, round dining tables, and high-backed chairs.

The influence of Mesopotamia

Furniture used by the Ancient Mesopotamians was similar to that of the Egyptians, albeit somewhat heavier and less ornate. Mesopotamian furniture design—with its notable use of decorative rings on chair legs and fringed cloth upholstery—**went on to influence Greek and Italian furniture**.

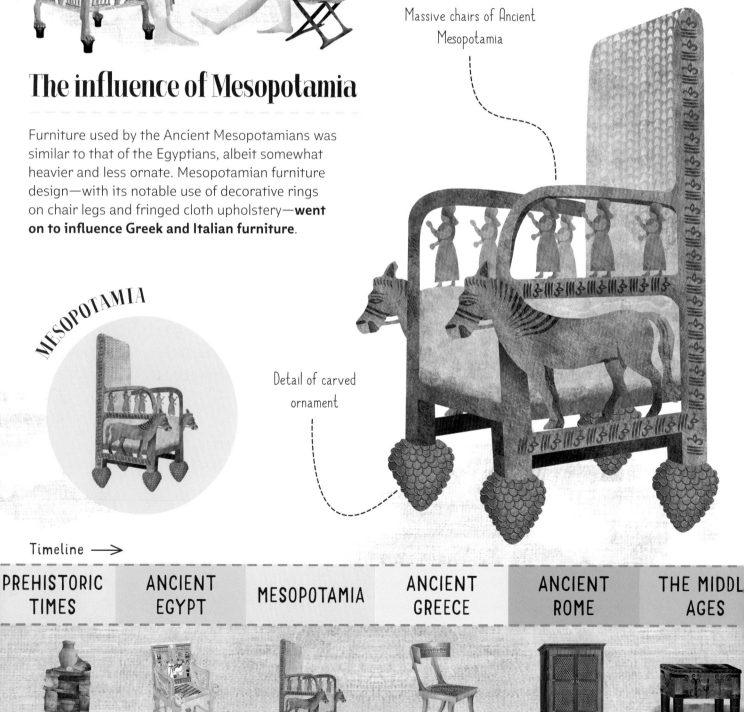

Massive chairs of Ancient Mesopotamia

MESOPOTAMIA

Detail of carved ornament

Timeline ⟶

PREHISTORIC TIMES	ANCIENT EGYPT	MESOPOTAMIA	ANCIENT GREECE	ANCIENT ROME	THE MIDDLE AGES

52

Marble chairs?

The houses of the Ancient Greeks were lightly furnished. As with Egypt, Greece used wood sparingly in the making of furniture, as it didn't possess a great deal of it. It is perhaps no wonder, then, that some Greek chairs were made of **marble** or **bronze**.

A light stool
diphros

ANCIENT GREECE

A marble bed

Comfortable
curved backrest

The klismos

Seats galore!

The simple, straight-backed chair was a Greek invention, and every household surely had at least one. The same could be said of the **diphros**: a light, four-legged stool with multiple uses, serving craftsmen as they worked, students in school lessons, and musicians as they played their instrument. The **klismos**—a chair with tapering, out-curved legs and a curved backrest—was no less popular as a comfortable seat.

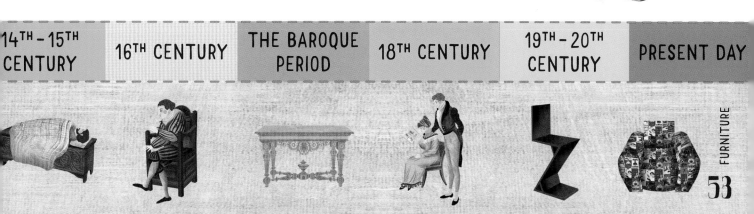

| 14TH – 15TH CENTURY | 16TH CENTURY | THE BAROQUE PERIOD | 18TH CENTURY | 19TH – 20TH CENTURY | PRESENT DAY |

FURNITURE

Oh, lie and eat ...

Today it is difficult to imagine eating lunch or dinner while lying down, but for the Ancient Greeks it was the most natural thing in the world. For this reason, all houses had dining couches, called **klinai**, for use at every dinner party. These were of ornate design and without a back—or armrests. At their narrowest point was a raised part for the head. Later klinai had a backrest, making them more like a modern-day sofa.

A well-deserved armchair

Magnificent armchairs and thrones were found only at the homes of the most important Greeks.

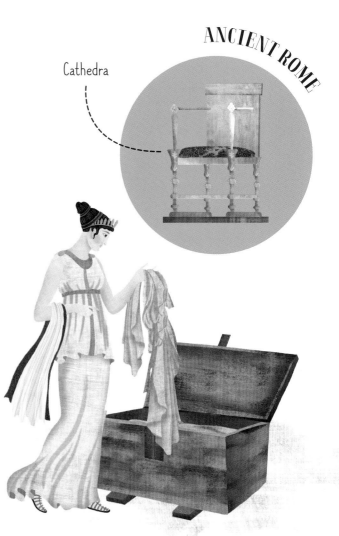

Cathedra

ANCIENT ROME

The joy of sitting

Sofas, chairs with and without arms, as well as backrests, stools, tables, **storage chests**, the first cupboards—if you visited an Ancient Roman family, you could admire all this. A bronze stool with an upholstered seat and a low base was a basic, very common item. The high chair known as the **cathedra** was used not only by teachers; it was common in the home too.

Timeline ⟶

| PREHISTORIC TIMES | ANCIENT EGYPT | MESOPOTAMIA | ANCIENT GREECE | ANCIENT ROME | THE MIDDL AGES |

Plus a table, of course

Now for the table. The tables used by the Romans were commonly round or rectangular, on three or four or armrests. At legs carved to resemble an animal's. The most popular materials were citrus wood and slate, although a **marble** table was nothing out of the ordinary and often found in gardens.

Roman marble table

Roman wardrobe

Chests, coffers, and cupboards

Although Romans stored much of their property in a cupboard known as an **armarium**, for the storing of their tunics, togas, and valuables they preferred **chests** and **coffers**. You could tell that a coffer was filled with treasures by the locks and metal mountings on it; some such coffers were firmly fixed to a stone base. As you can see, thieves didn't get much change out of wealthy Romans.

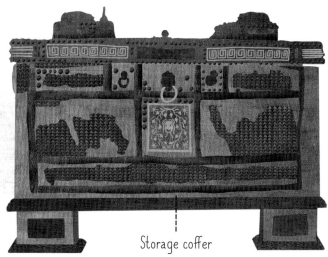

Storage coffer

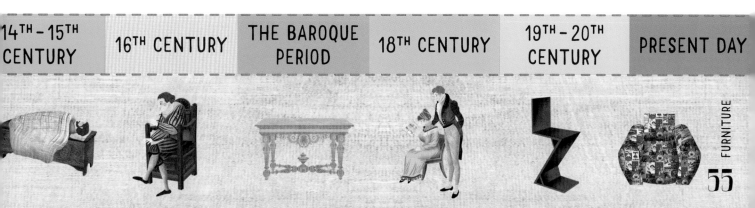

14TH – 15TH CENTURY | 16TH CENTURY | THE BAROQUE PERIOD | 18TH CENTURY | 19TH – 20TH CENTURY | PRESENT DAY

FURNITURE

Medieval = heavy

Unlike the furniture of ancient times, that of the early Middle Ages was **bulky** and **heavy**. In this period, furniture was sparse, and only the **most basic kinds** were used. Very little pre-14th-century furniture survives, owing to the rotting of wood and the fact that furniture was made in very small numbers.

A single chair—is that all there is?

Nothing but a fireplace, a table, a single chair (for the master), some benches and stools, and a few multi-functional packing cases—many a medieval room would have looked just like this. In this period, packing cases were a godsend. **First, they served as storage space; second, you could push a few of them together to make a bed and thus get a good night's sleep**. Oak was the basic material for furniture.

Timeline ⟶

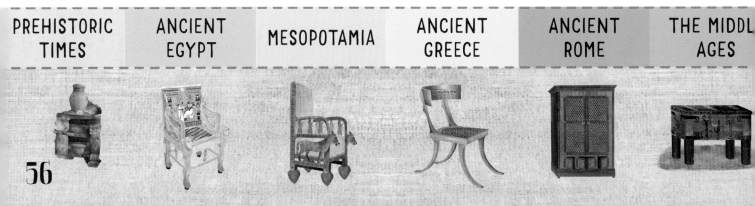

PREHISTORIC TIMES	ANCIENT EGYPT	MESOPOTAMIA	ANCIENT GREECE	ANCIENT ROME	THE MIDDL AGES

56

Voila! How practical!

Time passed and rich people extended their activities to include more than one house, thus creating a need for more furniture of different kinds. When nobles moved from their summer residence to their winter residence and vice versa, they took everything they had with them, including their furniture. This explains the popularity at that time of **folding chairs** and **stools** and **tables** and **cupboards** with **detachable panels**.

Packing case as a storage space

Packing case as a chair

Packing case as a bed

The unbeatable packing case

"You can't beat the good old packing case!" So went an adage of the Middle Ages, when cabinetmakers knocked out one packing case after another. The packing case was the true foundation of medieval furniture, serving as **coffer, cupboard, seat,** or **table**, depending on the need. By the end of the 15th century, however, it was losing ground to the newfangled wardrobe.

14TH – 15TH CENTURY	16TH CENTURY	THE BAROQUE PERIOD	18TH CENTURY	19TH – 20TH CENTURY	PRESENT DAY

Hand-me-down chairs

As in earlier times, in the 16th century furniture was a luxury item, so it was **passed down through the generations**. Although chairs were now quite common in the home, these chairs were nothing special. Typically, there were only three of them: one for the master of the house, one for his wife, and a third for their esteemed guest. Everyone else sat on a stool, or even on the floor.

Bombast or sobriety?

Forget about the Middle Ages and their limited range of furniture. Two styles run through the furniture of the 18th century: the highly **ornamental Rococo** and sober **Neoclassicism**. The progressive 18th century also saw the first **catalogues**, from which connoisseurs could choose furniture for their apartments and houses. This was when the history of named furniture-makers began. All this was of interest only to the wealthier classes, of course; the poor continued to take good care of the basic furniture handed down to them.

A flavor of the Orient

Seventeenth-century furniture fell for the **ornate style of the Baroque**. Bulky cupboards and commodes were varnished and—now that sea travel to Asia was the coming thing—adorned with **Oriental motifs**. Exotic woods such as mahogany and ebony began to compete with oak as the basic production material. At this time, chairs became a common item in every household. The 17th century came up with new pieces of furniture, notably the **bookcase**, the **commode**, and **impressive clocks**.

Thanks to catalogues, customers could choose new furniture from the comfort of home.

— Nice.

Timeline ⟶

PREHISTORIC TIMES	ANCIENT EGYPT	MESOPOTAMIA	ANCIENT GREECE	ANCIENT ROME	THE MIDDL AGES

Biedermeier

The 19th century brought the calm, conservative **Biedermeier** style of furniture to the homes of wealthy townspeople. Rooms carefully and tastefully furnished and fitted for the reception of guests were complemented by rooms in which the family would spend most of their time. These contained mahogany couches for relaxation, comfortable winged armchairs, round, one-legged tables, round-backed chairs, plus a new item of furniture known as a **cabinet**, where china, glass, and other decorative pieces were stored.

Glass cabinet with decorative items

Living room in Biedermeier style

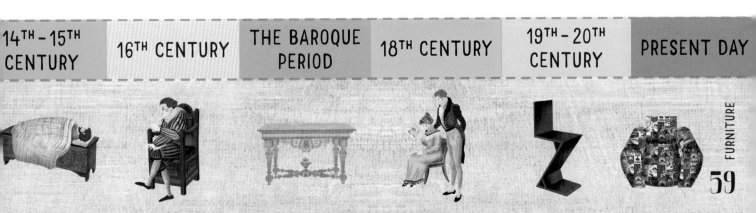

14TH – 15TH CENTURY	16TH CENTURY	THE BAROQUE PERIOD	18TH CENTURY	19TH – 20TH CENTURY	PRESENT DAY

De Stijl

From 1917 to 1931, a Dutch movement called De Stijl brought **abstract motifs** to furniture-making. Members of the movement **admired Cubism**, so unsurprisingly De Stijl's blue, yellow, and red armchairs look as though they have jumped from a Cubist painting. The furniture had clear, clean lines and a cheerful, unambiguous functionality.

20th century—new shapes and colors.

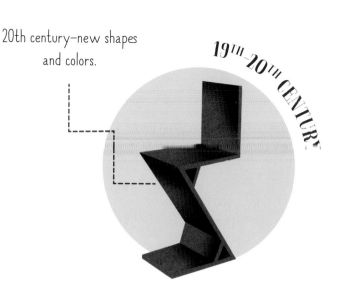

19ᵀᴴ–20ᵀᴴ CENTURY

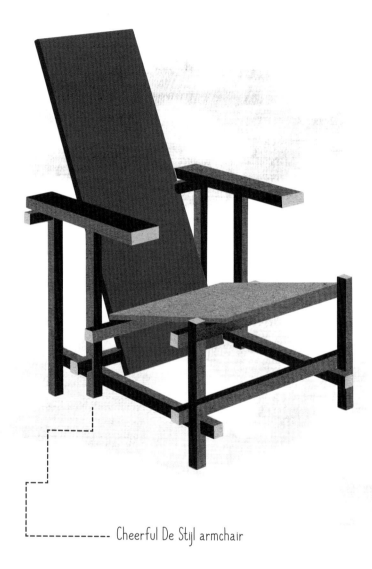

------- Cheerful De Stijl armchair

Art deco

Art deco is a style of visual arts from the first half of the 20th century that saw the creation of elegant furniture marked by **geometric simplicity** and playful use of color. Practitioners of art deco combined varnished wood (ordinary or Oriental) with gleaming chrome.

Timeline ⟶

| PREHISTORIC TIMES | ANCIENT EGYPT | MESOPOTAMIA | ANCIENT GREECE | ANCIENT ROME | THE MIDDLE AGES |

Ecodesign

If we want to be kind to nature, we shouldn't cut down trees to make chairs. This attitude marks a 21st-century trend in furniture-making. So which materials are used instead? One is cotton, as it is more considerate toward nature and the **atmosphere**. There was a time when the only things we inflated were swim rings and balloons. Today, **inflatable furniture** is trendy. Please take a seat at the world's most comfortable chair.

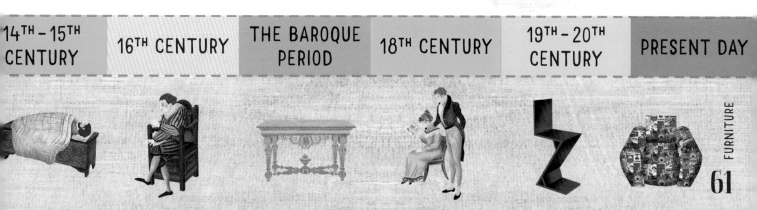

14TH – 15TH CENTURY	16TH CENTURY	THE BAROQUE PERIOD	18TH CENTURY	19TH – 20TH CENTURY	PRESENT DAY

FURNITURE

WALLPAPER

If you don't wipe that chocolate from your hands, you'll smudge the wallpaper. Your grandmother may have issued just such a warning, for fear that the cute little roses on her wall might be spoiled. Nice wallpaper adds a different dimension to a room, as well as evoking a sense of coziness. Let us now take a little trip through the history of wallpaper.

Colorful ancient times

We won't find the kind of wallpaper we know here either. But take a good look at the beautiful wall paintings of **scenes from Egyptian life and the hieroglyphs** that adorn the palaces and tombs of Ancient Egypt. Paintings in seven colors—blue, yellow, red, black, white, brown, and green—were found in even the dustiest corner.

Cave paintings

In prehistoric times, wallpaper was nonexistent, of course. For one thing, prehistoric humans knew nothing about paper, the base material. For another, wallpapering a cave would be an impossible task. But who is to say that we shouldn't consider the first **cave paintings** as distant ancestors of today's wallpaper? Although they had a distinctly ritualistic function, you can't deny that they gave a cave a certain pizzazz.

Timeline ⟶

PREHISTORIC TIMES	ANCIENT EGYPT	ANCIENT CHINA	ANCIENT GREECE AND ROME

China

The **earliest paper** was produced around 3,000 BCE from hemp. Later paper made use of silk and flax. The first wallpaper was produced in China around 200 BCE. The kind of paper we know today first saw the light of day in the 1st century AD, also in China.

Leather is unbeatable

As we continue our tour of the history of wallpaper, let us now leave prehistory and antiquity to skip to the heart of the Middle Ages. Can you imagine the stone walls of a medieval castle adorned with fine wallpaper with a subtle floral pattern? I thought not. That is because medieval walls were decorated with panels of **gilded leather**, stretched and mounted in wooden frames. Not only did this "wallpaper" improve the appearance of a room, but it also provided great insulation, thus keeping out the cold.

Antiquity

In antiquity, houses were decorated with murals (wall paintings). **Colorful mosaics** from the Orient were popular wall decorations, too. Human figures and/or flowers were common motifs of these mosaics. The Greek mosaic consisted mainly of colored stones, while the Roman mosaic made abundant use of colored glass and glass pegs.

THE MIDDLE AGES	THE RENAISSANCE	17TH – 18TH CENTURY	19TH – 20TH CENTURY

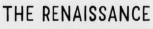

Tapestry

The tapestry can be considered another form of medieval "wallpaper." It is a **textile picture** that, like the leather panel, has a dual function: the first artistic, the second insulating. The art of tapestry-weaving came to Europe with the marauding Saracens. Some of the great names of painting from different periods, notably the Italian **Raphael**, the German **Albrecht Dürer**, and the Spaniard **Francisco Goya**, designed motifs for tapestries.

THE RENAISSANCE

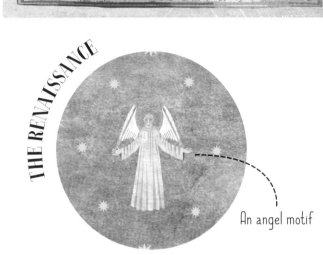

An angel motif

Renaissance angel

The painter **Jean Bourdichon** is inextricably linked with the Renaissance. In 1481, King Louis XI of France commissioned Bourdichon to paint 50 rolls of paper with a motif of **angels on a blue background** to decorate the royal residence, thus setting an example to his nobility, who began to order abundant supplies of wallpaper. Before then, papering walls was more popular with small merchants than aristocrats. The insides of cupboards, cabinets, and bookcases were papered at this time too.

Timeline ⟶

PREHISTORIC TIMES	ANCIENT EGYPT	ANCIENT CHINA	ANCIENT GREECE AND ROME

Wallpaper designs in the Renaissance

Flower and nature motifs in a symmetrical arrangement—this was the way to go for wallpaper during the Renaissance. Moorish ornamentation was also popular. In England, wallpaper was often adorned with a coat of arms or portraits of the wallpaper owner's aristocratic descendants. Ceilings, too, were wallpapered: typically in designs that imitated wood or carving.

Let's get printing!

French engraver and designer **Jean Papillon** is regarded as the inventor of patterned wallpaper. In 1688, he established a large factory to produce wallpaper. Papillon's son Jean-Michel continued where the father left off, achieving a continuous pattern through the use of block designs. This technique for printing wallpaper persisted well into the 18th century, despite its relatively high complexity and cost. Whereas we are used to pasting paper to the wall, in those days it would be attached by means of a hammer and copper nails.

Exotic imports

The 17th century saw a growth in demand for wallpaper **imported from China**. Made from fine mulberry paper, it was patterned with scenes from everyday life in China or motifs of exotic plants, birds, trees, rocks, and pagodas. Although Chinese wallpaper was relatively expensive, it sold like hot cakes. Paradoxically, the Chinese did not paper the walls of their homes; the wallpaper was produced for export only.

Jean Papillon
1639–1710

17TH–18TH CENTURY

Very popular oriental motifs

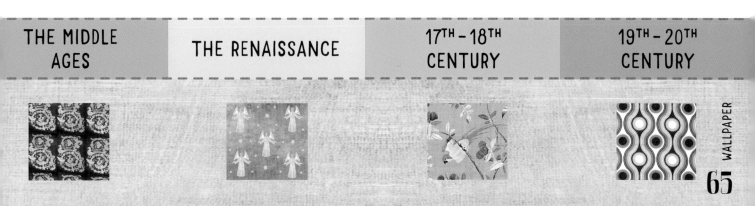

THE MIDDLE AGES	THE RENAISSANCE	17TH–18TH CENTURY	19TH–20TH CENTURY

The first wallpaper factory

Another century means a new name—this time that of **Jean-Baptiste Réveillon**. In addition to being the first French stationer to import wallpaper from England, Réveillon established his own wallpaper factory, using his dear wife's dowry. His wallpaper was characterized by its use of **velvet paper** printed in bright colors. Having produced **papier bleu d'Angleterre**, the paper that adorned the apartments of France's Queen Marie Antoinette, he became the exclusive supplier of wallpaper to the royal family. Anyone who was anyone had at least one room in their house decorated with wallpaper by Jean-Baptiste Réveillon.

Wallpaper production goes big!

In the 18th century, wallpaper-making became a matter of machine production. The first such machines were developed and operated in France. In 1788, France's King Louis XVI issued a royal decree stating that a length of wallpaper should be 30 feet long!

Baroque wallpaper motifs

At the beginning of the Baroque period, the most popular wallpaper motifs imitated wood, plaster, marble, brocade, and lace. Depictions of fierce hunting scenes were also much in demand. Before long, however, these motifs were replaced by depictions of flowers, vases, shells, and landscapes, and also by Chinese patterns. Bold colors gave way to pastel colors.

Wallpaper in rolls

The Age of Steam witnessed the dying days of wallpaper produced in printed sheets. From 1830, people could purchase wallpaper in **practical rolls** of the kind we know today. The consequent decrease in production costs resulted in the wide availability of wallpaper. From then on, wallpaper was no longer unusual. People began to merrily wallpaper their homes, with particular emphasis on the nursery.

Timeline ⟶

PREHISTORIC TIMES	ANCIENT EGYPT	ANCIENT CHINA	ANCIENT GREECE AND ROME

William Morris

One of the most **important English designers** of the 19th century brought about a revolution in wallpaper decoration. As an admirer of pure, natural beauty, William Morris adorned his wallpaper with subtly stylized plants commonly found in meadows and villages. After so many exotic-flower motifs, he felt it was time for a change.

The most common wallpaper motifs

In the 19th century, depictions of wood, stuccowork, textiles, and heraldry appeared on wallpaper, as did highly popular nature-inspired motifs, notably realistic flowers in bright colors. Eventually, motifs became heavily stylized.

Morris's wallpaper motifs

Wallpaper boom

In the 20th century, the floodgates opened for wallpaper production. Wallpaper was something everyone wanted. There was cheap wallpaper and expensive wallpaper, allowing the customer to choose according to their budget. Wallpaper patterns changed every decade or so, as **dictated by fashion**. Now floral patterns were the big thing, now geometric shapes were on trend. Motifs of Ancient Egypt gave way to abstract patterns and the bright-colored pop art of the 1960s.

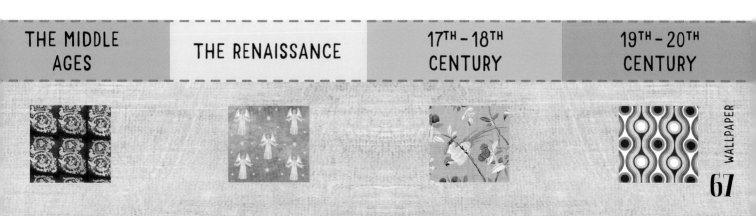

| THE MIDDLE AGES | THE RENAISSANCE | 17TH – 18TH CENTURY | 19TH – 20TH CENTURY |

BOARD GAMES

What could be better than sitting around the table with your mom and dad in the evening, drinking tea and playing a game? Chess, Ludo, *Monopoly*, cards, you name it—they are all great fun. But when did people begin to amuse themselves in this way? Well, let us see for ourselves how all this fun got started and how it developed.

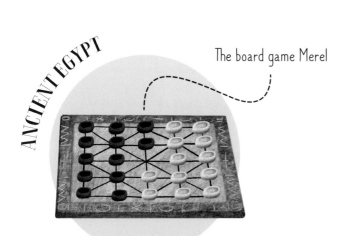

ANCIENT EGYPT

The board game Merel

Mehen

Mehen is the name of the snake who accompanied the Egyptian sun god Ra. The popular game of Mehen was coil-shaped, like the snake, and its pieces were shaped like lions or lionesses—for the game of Mehen represented a lion hunt. The dead snake was meant to be the lions' bait; the players, of whom there could be several, were **meant to be lion hunters**.

The first board games

If you believe that board games are a thing of recent decades only, what you are about to read will come as a big surprise. The very oldest such games were played in ancient times, around 4,000 BCE. In Egypt, archaeologists have found relics of games in the tombs of noble personages from antiquity, and the process of playing them is depicted on murals. Low- and high-born Egyptians alike played games to pass the time with entertainment. Also, game-playing was a good means of resolving arguments and disputes.

Timeline ⟶

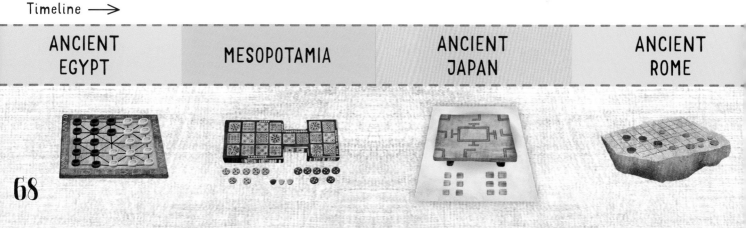

ANCIENT EGYPT	MESOPOTAMIA	ANCIENT JAPAN	ANCIENT ROME

Senet

Senet was a very popular Egyptian game that may have been played as early as 3,500 BCE. Its two players each sought to move their pieces as quickly as possible across three rows of ten squares, thus leaving Duvet (the kingdom of the dead), as symbolized by the playing area. The players relied on chance; moves were determined by throwing sticks or dice. Pieces could be knocked off the playing area. The first player to reach the end square (which was also the starting square) achieved rebirth. Finishing second meant eternal damnation.

Nobles also liked to play board games.

Alquerque and Merels

It is 1,400 BCE, and by this time the favorite games of the Ancient Egyptians are Alquerque and Merels. These two games would gradually spread across all Europe. **Alquerque** is the great-great-grandmother of checkers, while **Merels** is the great-great-grandfather of the game Nine Men's Morris. (It is said that nine men's morris originated out of the Irish Bronze Age game Three Men's Morris.)

Senet

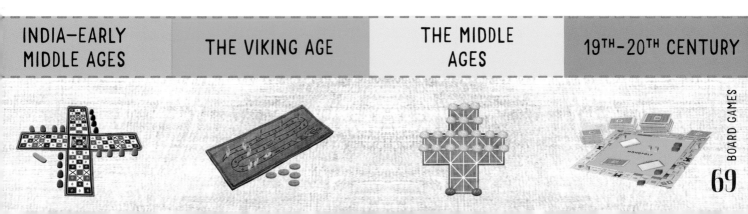

INDIA–EARLY MIDDLE AGES	THE VIKING AGE	THE MIDDLE AGES	19TH–20TH CENTURY

BOARD GAMES

69

Royal game

The influence of the popular Egyptian game Hounds and Jackals was clear in Ancient Mesopotamia around 2,600 BCE—in a game of **Wolves and Sheep**, played by Sumer royalty. In this game, players relied on the favor of the gods when they tossed three pyramid-shaped dice. Battle was done by seven black pieces and seven white pieces on a playing area of 20 squares. Some of these squares bore a picture of a rose, which probably allowed for an extra move. Archaeologists discovered this royal game in the tomb of Shubad, princess of Ur. So we know for sure that princesses have always enjoyed games.

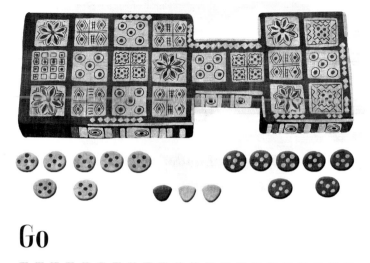

Go

One of the oldest games still popular today is Japan's **Go**, which was actually invented in China around 2,250 BCE, when it was known as **Weiqi**. Go is a game of strategy rather than chance. The moves of its black and white pieces do not result in a winner and a loser, making it a **game without an end**. The two players take turns placing their pieces on a 19 × 19 grid, the aim being to create a black or white territory of the greatest possible size. The game ends when one of the players concedes.

Liubo

This Chinese game goes back to 1,500 BCE. Wishing to show everyone that he was mightier than God, Emperor Wu Yi had a game made comprising one figure referred to as **God** and a second referred to as the **Emperor**. Out of respect for their lord, officials playing with the Emperor figure ensured that God was always defeated. The later Zhou dynasty had the two figures renamed. The word liubo means **"kill the general."** This game forms the basis of the Chinese chess game Xiangqi.

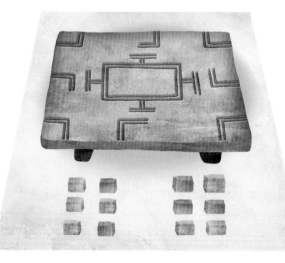

Timeline ⟶

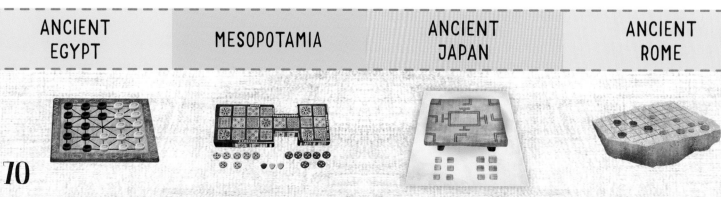

ANCIENT EGYPT	MESOPOTAMIA	ANCIENT JAPAN	ANCIENT ROME

Latrunculi

In Ancient Rome, game-playing was very popular among soldiers. After all, they had to find some way to pass the time before going to war! Latrunculi—also known as **"the legionnaire's life and death"**—was a typical soldiers' game. It simulated the clash of two armies and required players to use their knowledge of military strategy. The aim of the game was simple—to eliminate the enemy through **strategic and tactical thinking**.

Ludus Duodecim Scriptorum

This very popular Roman game originated in the 1st century BCE. It is related to the Egyptian game Senet and also to Backgammon. The board is composed of three rows, symbolizing past, present, and future. The dice represent the whims of fate and fortune. The players roll the dice as they try to move their pieces to the end of the playing area as quickly as possible. The first to reach it is the winner. The playing area was often decorated with **words of wisdom**.

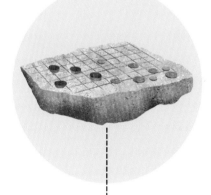

ANCIENT ROME

The strategic game Latrunculi

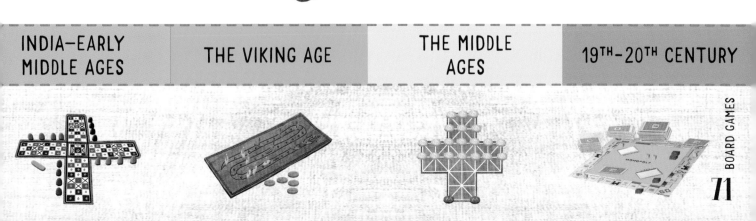

INDIA–EARLY MIDDLE AGES	THE VIKING AGE	THE MIDDLE AGES	19TH–20TH CENTURY

Backgammon

Fifteen pieces, four dice, strategy influenced by chance: these are components in another game **popular in Ancient Rome**, known as Backgammon. The players toss dice as they try to get their pieces home and thus off the board of play. The first player to do this is the absolute winner. Far from falling out of favor by the end of antiquity, Backgammon was played with great enthusiasm throughout the Middle Ages.

INDIA

I want to win!

Pachisi

This game, which we play today in a simplified form called **Ludo**, comes from 5th-century India. The moving pieces on the board were sometimes inanimate figures, sometimes living people. As the rules are much more elaborate than those of Ludo, it is popular with adults too.

Timeline ⟶

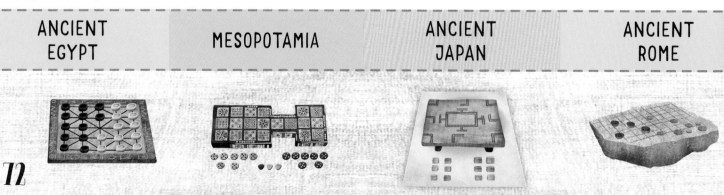

ANCIENT EGYPT	MESOPOTAMIA	ANCIENT JAPAN	ANCIENT ROME

Valhalla, the game of the Vikings

Even the super-tough Vikings liked to pass the time with a board game. One of their favorites was called Valhalla. **Each player** had six ships, which, by rolling runic dice, they aimed to **move across the seas and oceans to the Other Side**—Valhalla. On their way, they had to overcome obstacles in the form of rocks, tempests, and other whims of fate delivered by the runes.

I'll win next time.

Hurray, I won!

Tafl

Tafl was another tough Viking game. On an 11 × 11 board, four Vikings mounted an attack on the king and his retinue. The king stood at the center of the board surrounded by 12 pieces—his defenders, who tried to move him safely to the side of the board. There were two more attackers than defenders, their aim being to capture the king. To do this, they had to eliminate the defenders. This game of combat trained Viking warriors in **strategic thinking**.

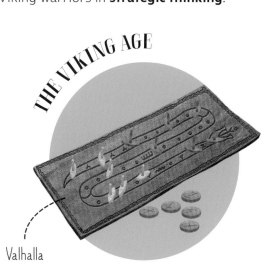

THE VIKING AGE

Valhalla

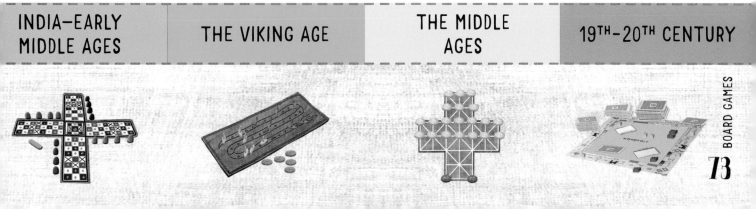

INDIA—EARLY MIDDLE AGES	THE VIKING AGE	THE MIDDLE AGES	19TH–20TH CENTURY

BOARD GAMES

Chess

India is the cradle of another hugely popular game—chess. It originated in the 6th century AD, when it was known as **Chaturanga**. One century later, the game was being played in Persia, in a slightly modified form, under the name **Chatrang**. Chess established itself in Europe in the 9th and 10th centuries. Records tell us that the first interstate chess tournaments were held in the 16th and 17th centuries.

Chess pieces

King   Queen   Bishop   Knight   Rook   Pawn

Chess

THE MIDDLE AGES

Two equally matched armies facing off on 64 squares

Aagh! Run for your lives!

Fox and geese

I'm terrifying when I'm hungry!

Fox and geese

Another game from the Middle Ages is called Fox and Geese. It originated in the 12th century, probably in England. It is played by two players on a board with five squares arranged in the shape of a cross. Sixteen pieces represent the geese, while two pieces represent the foxes. The geese try to pass from one side of the board to the other while blocking the foxes, whose aim is to attack them. The winning player **delivers the greatest number of geese to safety**.

Timeline ⟶

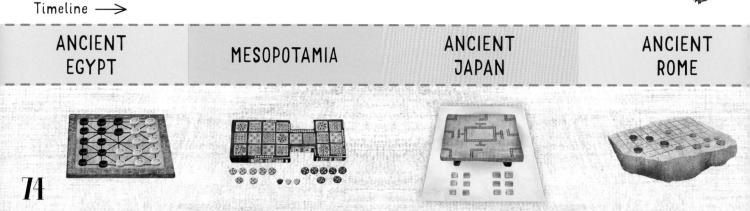

ANCIENT EGYPT   MESOPOTAMIA   ANCIENT JAPAN   ANCIENT ROME

Reversi (known as Othello)

The game Reversi, which we know today as Othello, was invented in 1888 by Englishmen **Lewis Waterman** and **John W. Mollett**. It is played on an 8 × 8 board with black and white game pieces. Players strive to compose long unbroken rows of pieces taken from the opponent. On taking an opponent's piece, the successful player turns it over so that it shows his own color. The winner has the greater number of pieces on the board.

Buying land and property

The 20th century was in its fourth year when US economist **Henry George** embarked on a futile struggle against speculators in real estate. Wishing to explain George's theories to the general public, his faithful admirer **Lizzie Magie** came up with *The Landlord's Game*. It is the game we know today as *Monopoly*. Although players of the game enjoy periods of wealth and hardship, Magie didn't make much money from her game, as she didn't mind that people copied her game in their own handmade versions.

How a pauper got rich

During the days of economic crisis, unemployed Charles Darrow of Pennsylvania staved off boredom by playing **Lizzie Magie's** game. As he did so, it occurred to him to try his luck by modifying the game and offering it for sale. Fortune favored him—the owner of the Parker Brothers company bought the game and had it patented. Just think of all the versions of and variations of *Monopoly* that have sold since!

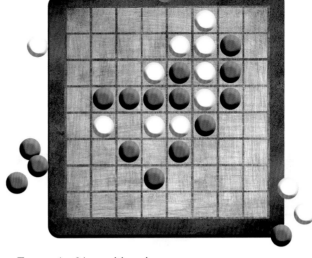

The point of Lizzie Magie's game was to teach the public to think in economic terms.

By modifying Lizzie Magie's game, Charles Darrow became a wealthy man.

INDIA–EARLY MIDDLE AGES

THE VIKING AGE

THE MIDDLE AGES

19TH–20TH CENTURY

BEDROOM

A room whose centerpiece is a bed or multiple beds is known, of course, as a bedroom. Adults tend to like this part of their home, because for some reason they have no objection to sleep, and some of them may even enjoy it. Many children, however, are no fans of the bedroom—although some have a liking for their parents' big bed, not least for its use as a trampoline when Mom and Dad are out.

Ancient Greek bedrooms

The Ancient Greeks had bedrooms in their houses. They contained couch-like beds and simple cupboards or chests for clothes. Close to women's bedrooms were the sleeping rooms of their servants, which were without beds; servants slept on the floor. The master's bedroom, too, was surrounded by the sleeping rooms of his servants. **Bedrooms were usually on the second floor of the house**.

Ancient Egypt

There were a great many rooms in the multifunctional houses of the Ancient Egyptians, but none would put us in mind of the kind of bedroom we know today. **Everything**—reception of visitors, business deals, meetings, and gatherings—**went on everywhere**. In some places, there simply happened to be a bed or two.

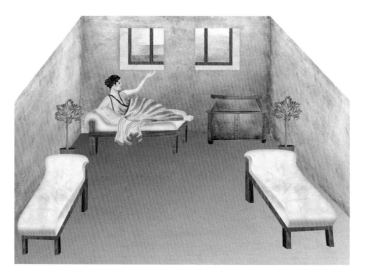

Timeline ⟶

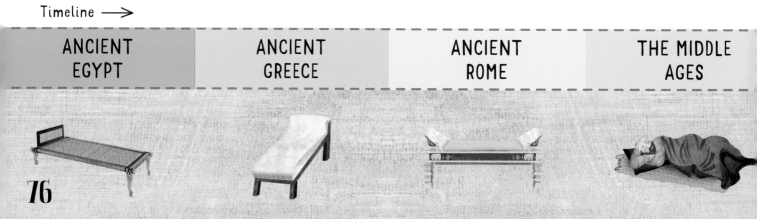

ANCIENT EGYPT	ANCIENT GREECE	ANCIENT ROME	THE MIDDLE AGES

Cubicula

The Roman bedroom—known as the **cubiculum**—was simply a place to lie down in of an evening and leave on waking in the morning. As a result, it was very small and sparsely furnished, even in the opulent homes of Rome's wealthiest. A bedroom known as **the cubiculum diurnum** served only for the midday siesta, so it was placed in the coolest part of the house. The Romans had a third type of bedroom too—**the cubiculum nocturnum**; this tended to be on the second floor in the west wing of the house, so that its occupants would be woken by the first light of day.

In the Middle Ages, not even the bedrooms of the wealthy and noble were strictly places of sleep. Located on the second floor of the house to keep them away from the hustle and bustle of the place, they served the function of VIP common room. Here, important events of the day were discussed, advantageous business deals were concluded, and last but not least, sleep was taken when tiredness set in.

Crowded bedrooms

As the Middle Ages weren't big on privacy, it will come as no surprise that there was no such thing as a private bedroom. **Everything took place in the house's main room, where the fireplace provided warmth**. It was here that people were born and died, where they feasted and mourned. Come evening, they would lie down on the ground, with a sack of hay as their bed and the warmth of the flames as their blanket.

16TH CENTURY	17TH CENTURY	18TH–19TH CENTURY	20TH CENTURY

Let's meet in the bedroom

The 16th century didn't change the way people regarded the bedroom. Although it contained a bed and clothing chest, **it was still a place for society**. Even in elevated royal circles, many important things happened in the bedchamber. Servants fought each other tooth and nail for positions in these rooms, for they were among the most privileged.

16th-century bedrooms were fully utilized.

The service in the bedrooms was one of the most privileged.

As well as sleeping in their bed, people dealt with important matters there.

Timeline ⟶

ANCIENT EGYPT	ANCIENT GREECE	ANCIENT ROME	THE MIDDLE AGES

Room for one more!

The bedroom of the 17th century was still very different from the bedroom of today. For one thing, it teemed with visitors and life. You might say it was bursting at the seams. Just imagine your bedroom as the place where you receive your **whole family**, plus various servants!

18TH–19TH CENTURY

Dressing table

Privacy at last!

Not until the 18th century did calmness and privacy enter the bedroom. **At last the bedroom was given its own door**, so that now it was a passageway no longer. Servants no longer lay at the foot of their masters' and mistresses' beds; now there were sleeping quarters for servants on the ground floor of the house. Tumultuous negotiations, contracts, and important political decisions left the bedroom—for the first parliaments, for instance.

16TH CENTURY	17TH CENTURY	18TH–19TH CENTURY	20TH CENTURY

BEDROOM

79

We poor have
but one room

Poor people of the day could only envy the luxury
of the private bedroom. The many members of the family
lived in a single room, where they had no choice but
to cook, wash, work, and sleep.

A ban on work in the bedroom

Complete privacy came to the bedroom in the 19th century. Each member of the household had his or her own bedroom: there was one for the mistress, one for the master, separate bedrooms for the children, even bedrooms for servants. Industrial progress and reductions in the cost of materials were reflected in the decoration of bedrooms—in the form of embroidered covers, heavy drapes at windows, modern furniture, and super-modern blinds. A washbasin and a dressing table still stood in the corner of the room.

Hollywood

The 1920s were marked by industrial development, economic progress, and the magic of the first Hollywood movies. With the coming of revolutionary new technologies, life became simpler, and people had more time for themselves. This time is marked, too, by **the final separation of bedroom and bathroom**, with the result that the bedroom became a charming place for rest and sleep only. Just to think that a few years earlier, the decisions of government had been made in it!

Timeline $\longrightarrow$

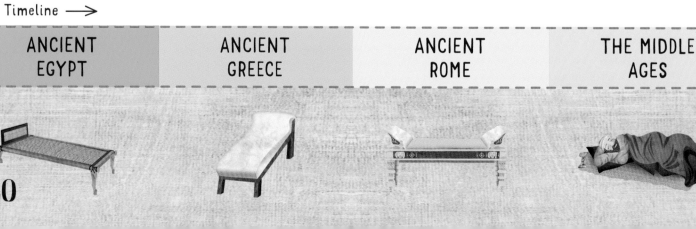

| ANCIENT EGYPT | ANCIENT GREECE | ANCIENT ROME | THE MIDDLE AGES |

Beauty in simplicity

There is beauty in simplicity, the 1960s screamed. Homemakers threw the counterpanes, blankets, and eiderdowns from their beds and replaced them with a modern Scandinavian invention—a one-piece quilt that made bed-making an effort-free task. **The acceptance of simplicity, comfort, and individuality would go on to inspire other new bedroom trends.**

16ᵀᴴ CENTURY	17ᵀᴴ CENTURY	18ᵀᴴ–19ᵀᴴ CENTURY	20ᵀᴴ CENTURY

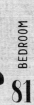

DOORS AND LOCKS

All living rooms, bathrooms, kitchens, bedrooms, and chambers in a home, be they large or small, are protected by a door with a proper lock. There is no chance of any uninvited, undesirable stranger getting in to enjoy your possessions. But what were the first doors and the first locks like? How did our ancestors protect their privacy?

In prehistoric times, an animal skin was hung over the mouth of a cave to make a door..

PREHISTORIC TIMES

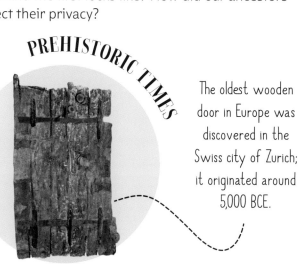

The oldest wooden door in Europe was discovered in the Swiss city of Zurich; it originated around 5,000 BCE.

Doors of leather

At the dawn of human history, a hut was protected against uninvited guests by a primitive "door" made of **animal skin** and some other **tough material**. The privacy of a dead Ancient Egyptian pharaoh was protected by an **impregnable stone door**; once this door was closed, no one would ever get it open again. A little later, the Ancient Greeks and Romans protected their dwellings with doors of **wood**, **bronze**, or **marble**. Wood has been the most popular material for doors for a very, very long time.

Egyptian barrier

The first lockable door was in Ancient Egypt. Although it was nothing sophisticated, its **ingenious mechanism of various latches** served its purpose to excellent effect—for only the owner of the key could open it. This key was a wooden bar whose pins fitted perfectly in their respective holes. Click, and the door was locked. The lock-and-key system is beautifully simple indeed! While the Egyptians toiled away with their wooden bars, the Chinese were opening their dwellings with real keys in real locks as early as 6,000 BCE!

ANCIENT EGYPT

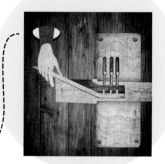

Only the owner of the right key could open this wooden bar, whose pins fitted snugly in their holes.

Timeline ⟶

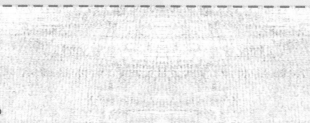

Hero of Alexandria

This brilliant Ancient Greek thinker came up with the first **automatic door**, an event that dates all the way back to the 1st century AD. This was not the door to a private home, however, but the spectacular entrance to a temple. Imagine the amazed faces of the faithful when the doors opened on their own, right in front of them! The mechanism of the automatic door was a simple one. It consisted of a hydraulic system that displaced water, thus mysteriously opening twin doors. **Hero**, who lived from 10 – 70 CE, was very much more than the inventor of the automatic door; he was also a mathematician, the director of the Musaeum at Alexandria, and an expert on mechanics and optics.

Robert Barron with his tumbler lock

Joseph Bramah

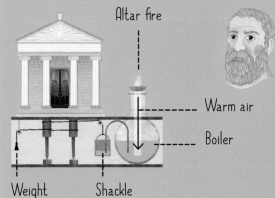

Hero of Alexandria's automatic door

Altar fire

Warm air

Boiler

Weight   Shackle

The warm air from the altar fire pushed part of the water from the boiler into the shackle, which opened the door with its weight. After extinguishing the sacrificial fire, the air cooled and the water flowed from the shackle back into the boiler by the action of a vacuum. The weight raised the shackle to its original height when closing the door.

Barron and Bramah

In 1778, Englishman **Robert Barron invented and patented the tumbler lock**. Six years later, his compatriot **Joseph Bramah** patented an improved lock on the same principle. In 1790, a challenge was declared: whosoever got Bramah's lock open would win a prize of 200 guineas. Sixty years would pass before the lock was defeated—by a clever American locksmith called **Alfred Hobbs**, with a picklock of his own design. Even so, the cracking of the lock took Hobbs 51 hours of work spread over 16 days. **Bramah's invention marks the beginning of the modern era of security locks**.

ANCIENT GREECE

18TH CENTURY

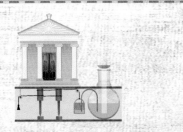

ENCYCLOPEDIA
OF ORDINARY
LIVING

© Designed by B4U Publishing for Albatros,
an imprint of Albatros Media Group, 2022
5. května 1746/22, Prague 4, Czech Republic
Printed in Czech Republic by TNM Print, s.r.o.
Written by Štěpánka Sekaninová
Illustrated by Eva Chupíková
Translated by Andrew Oakland
Edited by Scott Alexander Jones

www.albatrosbooks.com

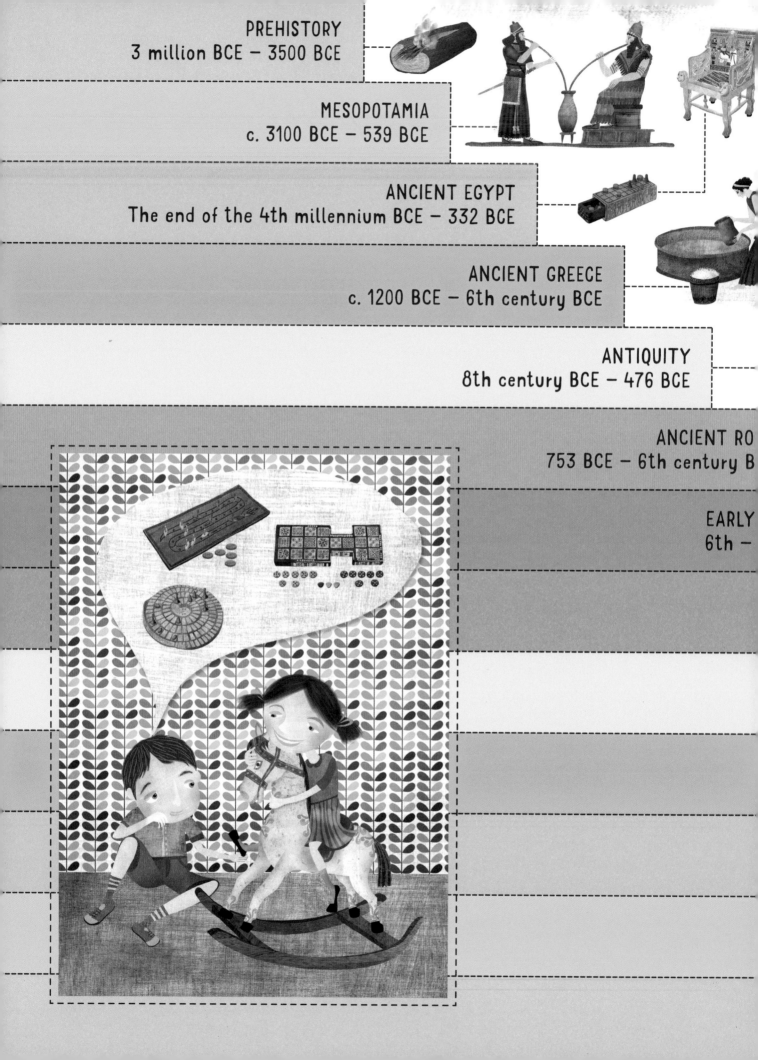

PREHISTORY
3 million BCE – 3500 BCE

MESOPOTAMIA
c. 3100 BCE – 539 BCE

ANCIENT EGYPT
The end of the 4th millennium BCE – 332 BCE

ANCIENT GREECE
c. 1200 BCE – 6th century BCE

ANTIQUITY
8th century BCE – 476 BCE

ANCIENT RO
753 BCE – 6th century B

EARLY
6th –